D1217414

DATE DUE			
FEB 24			
MAR 1 6			

LOCK, STOCK, AND BARREL

Books by Donald J. Sobol

The Double Quest
The Lost Dispatch
The First Book of Medieval Man
Two Flags Flying
A Civil War Sampler
The Wright Brothers at Kitty Hawk
The First Book of the Barbarian Invaders
Stocks and Bonds (with Rose Sobol)
Encyclopedia Brown, Boy Detective
An American Revolutionary War Reader
Lock, Stock, and Barrel

LOCK,
STOCK,
AND
BARREL

by
DONALD J. SOBOL

Illustrated by
EDWARD J. SMITH

THE WESTMINSTER PRESS · *Philadelphia*

LIBRARY OF CONGRESS CATALOG CARD No. 65-10364

PUBLISHED BY THE WESTMINSTER PRESS
PHILADELPHIA, PENNSYLVANIA ®
PRINTED IN THE UNITED STATES OF AMERICA

For Helen and Bob Lane

Contents

THOMAS GAGE

The Mild General

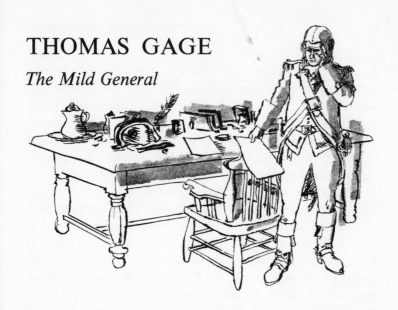

ON APRIL 14, 1775, A PINK-CHEEKED YOUNG BRITISH ARMY captain named Oliver De Lancey stepped from the gangplank of H.M.S. *Nautilus* onto Clark's Wharf in Boston. Past dripping hawsers, drying fish, sail lofts, and warehouses he hurried till at the corner of Fish Street he commandeered a horse and rode away at the fastest possible clip.

His destination was Province House, the three-story royal governor's mansion on Marlborough Street. A jump to the ground, a salute, quick steps, and he stood inside the oak-lined office of General Thomas Gage, commander of His Majesty's forces in America.

De Lancey bore a copy of "secret" orders—the original was to arrive two days later—from the British Cabinet. The two men chatted briefly; De Lancey withdrew, and Thomas Gage, dubbed the "Old Woman" by his officers and men, sat down with the parcel.

BORN: 1721 (?), Firle (?), England
DIED: April 2, 1787, Portland Place, England

He broke the seal and read. The words were sometimes scolding, sometimes encouraging, and always strained with impatience. The author, the Earl of Dartmouth, Secretary of State for the Colonies, demanded prompt action against the three New England colonies "determined to cast off their dependence." Dartmouth urged Gage to form a corps of Tories, and he informed the general that reinforcements were on the way from England.

Dartmouth again and again exhorted Gage to move vigorously and at once. In effect, the letter announced a vital decision: *the Cabinet had accepted the responsibility for using force.* Gage was rescued from his marvelous ballet. For a year he had tiptoed around using force on his own authority. If war came, he had held, the Americans or the home government must begin it.

Thomas Gage put down the letters, rose from his huge walnut desk, and stared meditatively out of a velvet-portiered window. Did the ministers have a true sounding of the rage of these people?

Unlike most British observers, Gage did not underestimate the queer-looking local militia, the pamphleteers, the orators. Repeatedly he had requested more troops to cope with the raw situation. He did not know that his letters never were shown to Parliament, where the colonies had many friends.

If the Crown determined not to yield to American demands, but to resist, Gage wanted that resistance to be overwhelming at the start. "If you think ten thousand men sufficient, send twenty," he had written. "You will save both blood and treasure in the end. A large force will terrify, and engage many to join you, a middling one will encourage resistance and gain no friends."

Slow-moving Thomas Gage may not have been England's most brilliant officer, but he understood the ugly mood of Americans in 1775. Eighteen of his thirty-five army years had been spent in the New World, the past twelve as Commander in Chief in America.

He had married a wealthy American girl, cousin to Philip Schuyler. All but one of their eleven children were born in America. He numbered George Washington (whom he would ever call *Mr.* Washington) among his many American friends.

Life had been sociable and seldom rippled until last year, when he had moved his headquarters. From hospitable Tory New York he had transferred to Boston, the frying pan of Whig unrest, and he had assumed the role of governor of Massachusetts. Still, he had preferred being the number one general in the colonies to the ninth- or tenth-ranked in England.

And now, suddenly, being ranked tenth in England and *being in England* looked delicious to middle-aged, peaceable Thomas Gage. He was feeling the crafty, lopsided pressure of Dartmouth's diplomatic squeeze. On one side was Dartmouth's promise of reinforcements, and on the other was Dartmouth's demand for immediate action.

From his "middling" Boston garrison of thirty-five hundred Redcoats, Gage detached his best companies under the subterfuge of learning "some new evolutions." Ever cautious, he postponed a mission of war pending the arrival of Dartmouth's original draft.

Meantime, he kept Boston in a mailed palm, if not a mailed fist. He maintained the sea blockade, already a year old, till the townspeople paid for the tea they had dumped. The blockade, a child of the Cabinet's, had tightened the unity of the Americans rather than weakened it. Gage had seen the food and money pouring into Boston from points as far away as South Carolina.

Such defiance of British authority upset him. Hadn't he always leaned backward to guard American rights under the English constitution? He had placed his officers, for the most part, in private dwellings, though under the Quartering Act he could lawfully lodge all his troops in homes. The bulk of his men camped in a hut village on Boston Common and in a distillery on Griffin's Wharf.

Yet the people derided his men as "lobster backs." Laborers dawdled on his fortifications. Ships bearing his supplies mysteriously sank, and his wagons overturned.

Around him the troops were wilting in a climate of hostility and inaction. Morale was low, desertions high, and temptations everywhere. A drunken or disgruntled Redcoat had no farther to look than his elbow for a buyer of his "Brown Bess"—four dollars for a clean musket, a dollar and a half for a rusty one. Gage had countered harshly: a firing squad for captured deserters, a hundred lashes for "losing" a flintlock. And he had stopped the traffic of farmers heading out of town with arms and ammunition hidden under a half wagonload of straw or manure.

Gage had done what he could to mend Britain's splintered authority. He had made sure that most of the Indians swore their hatchets to the service of the Crown. He had conducted drills in the form of long marches so that his men—and the people of Massachusetts—grew accustomed to treks into the country. He had kept himself informed of patriot movements through paid informers. He had even ventured shotless sorties to seize stores of powder and arms.

Lord Dartmouth's original draft arrived on April 16. Once assured that the earlier copy was true, that no slip of a clerk's quill might lead him into a ghastly mistake, Gage acted. On the morning of April 18 he sent out picked young officers to scout and secure key roads. In the afternoon he called in three of his most trusted senior officers.

Gage explained. The companies that had been learning new evolutions—ten of light infantry and eleven of grenadiers—were to be mustered on the Common at ten o'clock that night. Longboats would convey the force, some seven hundred men, across the Charles River. At embarkation time the three officers would learn their objective, and not before.

Lieutenant Colonel Francis Smith, one of the three, was given command. At fifteen minutes before ten, Gage handed him his orders. Smith opened the stiff parchment and read it under the bright candlelight of the crystal chandelier hanging above the walnut desk.

The objective was Concord. The purpose, to "seize and destroy all Military Stores. . . . But you will take care that the Soldiers do not plunder the Inhabitants . . ."

After Smith's departure, Thomas Gage was left to pace his office. No man in all the continent was more terribly alone. He could tell himself he had done all that was humanly possible to give the spirit of rebellion time to quiet down. Now he had cast his hand, and the horrible dice of war were clanking and rolling toward Concord.

Would the Americans fight? By midnight there was no doubt. Church bells pealed, drums beat, and shots were fired to awaken the countryside. The march was no secret. Messengers had somehow got through his sentries to sound the alarm.

Gage stripped Boston of a brigade and dispatched it to Smith's support. The relief column saved Smith's returning detachment from merciless slaughter by the minutemen.

But April 19, 1775, was a sorry day for the British army. A meager amount of munitions—what the rebels had not hidden—was destroyed. The cost was 73 killed, 174 wounded, 26 missing, and the ultimate loss of the American colonies.

King George III liked Gage, his "Mild General," and he refused to brand him with the stigma of dismissal. In December, 1774, he had decided to send three major

generals—Howe, Clinton, and Burgoyne—as helpers.
They arrived in May. In September, three months after
the dubious victory at Bunker Hill, Gage was recalled to
England. He was given a promotion but never again a
field command.

Governor John Wentworth of New Hampshire summed
up Gage's career in America. The governor's words are
very probably the understatement of the eighteenth
century.

Thomas Gage, wrote Wentworth, was "a good and
wise man . . . surrounded by difficulties."

PAUL REVERE
The Midnight Rider

THERE WERE THOSE IN BOSTON WHO KNEW THAT THE time had come when, shortly after dusk on April 18, 1775, a small band of picked British officers trotted out of town.

The well-mounted, well-armed Redcoats chattered cheerily about taking the country air. At the stables, however, they had been overheard talking in quite a different mood. They had jested about the fur to fly tomorrow.

Later that evening some of the King's crack units were detached from their regiments. Singled out were big, heavy-duty grenadiers and several companies of swift-flanking light infantry.

Footsteps, secrecy, and the clink of muskets mingled at the edges of Boston. The thriving port of fifteen thousand danced with rumors.

For burly Paul Revere, master silversmith, the time

BORN: January 1, 1735, Boston, Mass.
DIED: May 10, 1818, Boston, Mass.

came at ten o'clock. To his house on North Square stole an unknown visitor. Urgent knocks brought the oaken squeak of a door, the flare of lamplight beneath the second-story overhang, the exchange of whispers.

As the visitor had bid him, Revere departed within a few minutes for Hanover Street. He walked quickly, though without appearing to hurry, to the fashionable home of Dr. Joseph Warren. The two men were fast friends. Their common opposition to overseas rule bridged the wide gap in their social positions.

Warren was thirty-four, handsome, Harvard-educated, an idealist doomed to die at Bunker Hill. Revere was forty, practical to his blunt fingertips, one of the organizers of a ring of artisans who kept tabs on the doings of the Tories and British troops billeted in town.

Warren knew about the troop movements. He surmised the British objectives: the seizure of rebel military stores at Concord seventeen miles away, and the capture of John Hancock and Sam Adams, two leading Sons of Liberty, who were "hiding" in Lexington.

Hancock and Adams had to be warned. The munitions had to be transferred to a safer point of concealment.

Warren told Revere to ride immediately through the British sentries by way of Charlestown and spread word of the British intentions. He had already sent another messenger, William Dawes, a cordwainer, to Lexington by the overland route across Boston Neck.

Having left Dr. Warren, Revere sought out young Robert Newman. Revere instructed him to hang two lanterns, a signal to Whig leaders in Charlestown. The previous Sunday, the silversmith had told Colonel William Conant, a high-level Whig, that he would signal if the British actually planned to use force to suppress the rebels. One lantern in the highest window arch of the North Church belfry would mean the British were marching by land. Two lanterns would mean they were moving across the Charles River to start from Charlestown.

As Robert Newman prepared to haul his two lanterns up past the eight huge church bells, Revere returned home. He donned overcoat and riding boots. Now he began to execute a plan of action laid out three days before.

He kept a boat hidden on the north side of town. On his way to it he was joined by his oarsmen, Joshua Bentley and Thomas Richardson. At the river they realized that the splashing of oars would give the business away. One of the oarsmen had a girl friend who lived at a nearby corner. He whistled beneath her window and explained. Off flew her flannel petticoat—O lost and nameless heroine!— and she dropped the garment into his waiting hands.

With oars muffled, the boat crossed the river between Boston and Charlestown, skirting the sixty-four guns of the British frigate *Somerset*.

Colonel Conant and a group of Whigs met Revere in the town. They had seen his signal lanterns, but they bore hard news. Heavy British patrols were already abroad, isolating Boston from the countryside. The odds were long against getting through to Lexington.

While the men huddled, discussing the perils, wealthy John Larkins' favorite horse, the mare Brown Beauty, was led out. Revere adjusted the stirrups. Patiently he checked the bridle and girths with the thick, sensitive fingers that had hammered out the best silverware made in America. His broad palm stroked the mare's arched neck and swelling muscles. A good mount was this horse of Larkins'—a "very good" horse, her grateful rider remembered years later.

The men fell silent. Revere lifted a boot into the stirrup. His gaze clung a moment to the spire-pricked skyline of Boston. The night was cold and clear and moonlit. The roads stretched like bars of silver. Lacy shadows and leafless spring trees offered scant comfort to a horseman in need of cover.

There was going to be shooting and death out beyond the warm houses, out where the cold moors and clay ponds and salt marshes lay. The stocky, middle-aged rider risked everything—business, wife, and a houseful of children—for a belief.

His hesitation was short-lived. An experienced express rider for the rebels, he knew the dangers ahead perhaps better than anyone. He swung into the saddle, the reins lightly gripped in his powerful hands. His spurs flashed inward.

It was eleven o'clock. Within five hours the ride was done. He had aroused "almost every house" on the way to Lexington; he had warned Hancock and Adams to flee; he had dodged bullets and deceived the Redcoats. That he was stopped before reaching Concord is a trifling misfortune. For Paul Revere, in a sense, is riding still.

With the outbreak of shooting, Revere, a marked man, was cut off from Boston and his business. For a time he rode for the rebels, doing their "outdoor business" at five shillings a day to support his family. Soon his talents were better employed. He made gunpowder and the first Continental paper money issued. He cut the first official seal of the colonies and the seal for the state of Massachusetts.

Although a fighter, he was not a soldier. True, in 1756 he had run off exuberantly to join the battle against the French-held fort of Crown Point. His Revolutionary career, however, passed largely in boring garrison duty.

Commissioned a major, he rose no higher than lieutenant colonel. He commanded Castle Island and served as second-in-command of the defenses of Boston, to which fighting never returned after Bunker Hill.

He learned to cast and repair cannon, and so was given command of the artillery in the ponderous, hapless attack on a small British naval base at Penobscot Bay in the summer of 1779. During the fiasco, Revere was charged falsely with insubordination and cowardice, and he lost his commission. For nearly three years he fought to obtain the court-martial that eventually exonerated him.

After the war the pace of life quickened. The day of the slow, careful workman at his bench was passing. Revere had been a jack-of-all-trades. For a time he had done engravings and manufactured false teeth (your choice of hippopotamus tusk or sheep's tooth). He had created and repaired whatever his customers demanded. A civilian again, he soon abandoned shopkeeping. He did not, though, ever abandon making his gracefully simple silverware despite the changing fads of the century.

He enlarged his activities. He became interested in bells. With his son he cast nearly four hundred. Some are still in use, ringing worshipers to church from the West Indies to Quebec.

He discovered a way to roll copper into sheets. Although sixty-five, he invested "every farthing" he could scrape together and built a mill. He produced boilers for Robert Fulton's ferry, put copper bottoms on American ships, and founded a sprawling modern industry.

He had eight children before his first wife died, and eight more by his second. He prospered and accepted the civic duties that accompany financial success. He served as coroner, jury foreman, grand master of Masons. He laid cornerstones and started a fire insurance company.

In later years he continued to delight in making superb silver, in casting bells, in fitting ships with copper, and in his abundant family.

As an honored, elderly citizen in the quaint, tight clothes of Revolutionary days, he walked the streets of a new Boston. Hills were leveled and land pushed out where once the sea had rippled beneath the glimmer of two lanterns.

He died at eighty-three. Not for another half century would Longfellow's poem replace the fine old gentleman with the symbol—the pounding hoofs of a phantom steed, the knock on the door, and the cry of alarm forever hung amid the moon dust of a great night.

ETHAN ALLEN
Green Mountain Giant

TWO WEEKS AFTER LEXINGTON A GROUP OF PATRIOTS visited a tavern in the wilds of the New Hampshire Grants. The good, sober gentlemen had journeyed up from Hartford to offer a chance at reputable warfare to a private army—a mob of rowdy, backwoods vigilantes known as the Green Mountain Boys.

What was wanted of the brawling mountain men was the capture of Fort Ticonderoga, back door to the colonies from British Canada. The delegation brought authority from Connecticut for the attack, fifty reinforcements, and three hundred pounds in cold cash.

The cash and a liberal pouring of stonewalls (a local drink of rum diluted by rock-hard cider) clinched the deal. The Connecticut men stepped from the taproom unsteadily, but happy in the success of their mission.

Towering Ethan Allen waved them good-by from the dooryard. Beside him rose a pine pole, twenty feet high.

BORN: January 10, 1737 (?), Litchfield, Conn.
DIED: February 12, 1789, Burlington, Vt.

On top crouched a stuffed catamount, facing New York, its teeth bared in a permanent snarl.

The big cat was the emblem of the tavern. It might easily have represented the untamed spirit of Allen and his neighbors in the Grants. They held their lands under grant of New Hampshire. The governor of New York claimed the Grants (modern Vermont) and sent in Yorkers as settlers and surveyors. Allen and his friends had organized in defense of their rights. His taproom cronies changed their name from the Bennington Mob to the Green Mountain Boys, and chose Allen as colonel commandant. Their private war had raged for five years.

Bashing Yorkers and chasing them back over the border, good clean fun though it had been, was laid aside for the Fort Ticonderoga adventure. Allen climbed on a table. "We're going on a big wolf hunt!" he bellowed.

The leather-lunged giant had a mind to match his self-confidence. In the briefest time he put together a plan to take the fort.

As the party tramped north, Allen called in more Green Mountain Boys. He collected a company of semi-outlaws like himself. They were rough-and-tumble fighters who ate meat for breakfast, signaled each other with three mournful hoots of an owl, and could shoot a nut from between a squirrel's jaws.

Outsized Ethan Allen could outthink, outfight, and outcurse them all. Probably no other man would have dared to take so unruly a pack of farmers, trappers, hunters, and woodsmen, and throw them into an attack upon a fort manned by trained soldiers.

Allen posted guards on the passes leading to the fort "to cut off all intelligence between the garrison and country." On the night of May 9–10, 1775, he advanced his two hundred and thirty men to Hand's Cove, within two miles of the fort by water. Here he received the report of his spy, Noah Phelps.

Phelps had entered the fort by posing as a simple woodsman in search of a barber. The fort, he reported, was in need of repairs. A "capital breach" existed in the south curtain. The Redcoats numbered fewer than fifty.

This good news was followed by two pieces of bad news. First, dawn neared and the boats to ferry the task force had not arrived. Second, Colonel Benedict Arnold burst out of the timber and proclaimed himself in command of the expedition.

Arnold had not a man except his valet. He had, however, the authority of Massachusetts, a splendid uniform, and a consuming self-interest. Ethan Allen had the authority of Connecticut, and all the fighters.

After a heated row, Allen agreed to compromise. Colonel Arnold would accompany him, shoulder to shoulder but in silence. The arrival of two boats, stolen downshore, probably influenced Allen. With light coming on, there was no time for a spat.

Allen loaded the boats to the gunwales with eighty-three of his men, and the invasion armada floundered across the wind-chopped Lake Champlain. The men debarked at Willow Point, out of sight of the fort.

After brushing aside another of the "damned rascal's" (Arnold's) demands to lead, Allen formed his men, ripped off a pep talk, and led them past the east wall of the fort. In the south wall he located the ruined spot that Phelps had reported. Drawing his long sword, he jumped inside, and charged a single dozing sentry.

The startled soldier raised his musket. It misfired, flashing in the pan. He whirled and raced for his life onto the parade ground.

The Green Mountain Boys poured in, howling, "No quarter!" and whooping like Mohawks. They sprinted

about the barracks, pounding doors and dragging out
Britishers. Allen spotted a soldier in the act of wounding
one of his men. He fetched the Redcoat a swipe on the
skull with the flat of his sword.

Before the dazed man could scramble away, Allen
gripped him by the hair and demanded to know where the
commanding officer slept. The terrified soldier pointed
to stairs in front of a barrack. Allen bounded up them,
bumping Benedict Arnold every step of the way.

Lieutenant Jocelyn Feltham, second-in-command,
emerged carrying his breeches. He stared at the charging
pair and with historic aplomb asked by what authority
His Majesty's fort was invaded.

Ethan Allen reared back, took a deep breath, and
roared, "In the name of the Great Jehovah and the Continental Congress!"

Feltham found the words and the spectacle fantastic.
He stalled. Allen waved his sword. He prepared to batter
down the door behind the lieutenant when Captain William
Delapace, commander of the fort, stepped out. Delapace
blustered a second or two, and surrendered.

Fort Ticonderoga and all the rum in its cellars belonged
to the Green Mountain Boys.

The bloodless (typical of Allen) fall of Ticonderoga
marked the first offensive launched by the rebels. Lexington
and Concord had been defensive actions, and both had
failed. It is true that the fort had decayed since a skeleton
force of French defenders had routed fifteen thousand
Britishers there during the French and Indian War in
1758. Nevertheless, it was the best-known fortress in the
colonies and contained valuable cannon. Allen's victory
thrilled the rebels.

The Ticonderoga exploit transfixed Ethan Allen in the
tapestry of the Revolution: a half-wild giant, sword in
hand, standing on the barrack steps, and shouting of the

Great Jehovah. As a staircase figure, he has neither past nor present. Yet he was, man and boy, many things: farmer, ironmaster, diplomat, author, deist, and founding father of Vermont.

Above all, he was a free man, in his religion, in his thinking, in his living. After Ticonderoga he joined the rash venture against Montreal. Captured, he spent two years in prison, much of the time in chains.

General Washington talked with him after his release. "His fortitude and firmness seem to have placed him out of the reach of misfortune," commented the Commander in Chief. "There is an original something in him that commands attention."

As a youth growing up in Connecticut he had caught deer by simply running them into exhaustion. All his life he was fond of performing—and roaring about—his feats of strength.

A champion curser, he could freeze even his roof-raising Green Mountain Boys in rapt appreciation. Because of his profanity, he had been invited to leave the town of Northampton, Connecticut, back in 1767. Outnumbered by more than he could fight or curse down, he had departed.

When it suited him, Allen shifted artfully from his backwoods character to orator and diplomat. In 1779 he was given command of the militia of the pretended state of Vermont, and he seems to have aimed his men mainly against his pet targets, Yorkers. Normally he outsmarted these city slickers, preferring bluff over violence. If he burned the houses of the stubbornest Yorkers, he only *promised* to leave everyone a corpse on his next visit.

After 1780 he took no part in the Revolution. He gave himself to his farm and Vermont affairs. He lobbied in Congress, flirted with Britain, and was instrumental in establishing the independent republic of Vermont. He penned a war memoir, *The Narrative of Colonel Ethan Allen*, which has sold briskly since 1779. His *Reason, the Only Oracle of Man*, appeared in 1784, the first American book to oppose revealed religion.

He died two years before Vermont became the fourteenth state. No portrait of him survives, and that is well. Ethan Allen could never be reduced to a painted figure.

He was one of God's unique creatures, and wherever men of courage, humor, and independence fight for their rights, there his spirit moves.

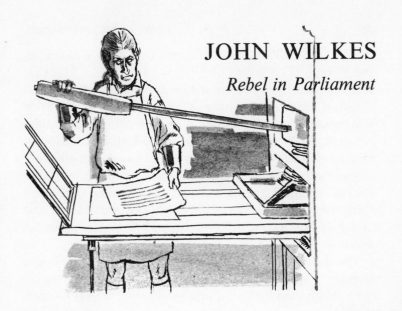

JOHN WILKES
Rebel in Parliament

THE DEVIL'S COSTUME FIT THE BABOON EXQUISITELY.

John Wilkes coaxed his counterfeit demon into a specially constructed black box, deftly slipped the rope from its neck, and slammed the lid.

Then Wilkes leered with appropriate fiendishness as he anticipated the night's prank.

Outside, twilight burned the cobbles of London. Had passersby spied Wilkes heaving his box into a hackney, they might have cried, "Wilkes and Liberty!" or thrown rotten eggs. Neither friend nor foe, however, would have been surprised that the demagogue had chosen to associate with a monkey.

Wilkes was a volcano of nonconformity. He lived and fought by his own convictions and was puppet of no man, least of all the King. As an editor and a member of Parliament, he made a career of hounding His Majesty. By 1763, the year of the weird episode now unfolding, he had also begun a lifetime of after-dark debauchery.

BORN: October 17, 1727, Clerkenwell, England
DIED: December 26, 1797, London, England

Had John Wilkes possessed a spotless private character and George III a sullied one, observed Benjamin Franklin, Wilkes might have run the monarch out of England.

Wilkes alighted from the hackney at High and West Wycombe Streets. He hauled his boxed companion up the hill to St. Mary's Abbey, an odd-shaped edifice restored by Sir Francis Dashwood to consecrate his worship of pleasure.

Through gardens planted with appropriate statuary Wilkes struggled till he reached the temple. Within an hour his fellow revelers, the self-styled "monks of the Order of Medmenham," had assembled. Wilkes bided his moment.

The profane rituals succeeded merrily. At midnight Horatio Walpole advanced through the flickering shadows of torchlight and intoned a prayer to Satan. Wilkes released the baboon.

For a ghastly instant the monks were smitten sober by the terrifying belief that the prayer had been answered. The short-tailed "Satan" pounced upon the back of Walpole, who subsided in a paroxysm of horror.

Hopping off the prostrate figure, the baboon leaped about with diabolic speed and escaped. For several days it unsettled the neighborhood. A furor of indignation broke upon the abbey, compelling the monks to give up their orgies.

Wilkes shrugged off the loss. Many of the monks were gentlemen, wealthy and influential, and though Wilkes continued on friendly terms with them, he regarded them as paralyzing bores in genteel society. His own descent into their evil order dated from the breakup of his marriage five years earlier.

"To please an indulgent father," he wrote, "I married a woman half as old again as myself; of a large fortune— my own being that of a gentleman."

After he parted from his wife, he pursued the gentle sex

tirelessly, calling upon his enormous charm to overcome the handicaps of his goggle eyes and twisted mouth. He had learned to treat his ugliness like a controlled experiment. "It takes me half an hour to talk away my face," he used to say.

Except in the realms of love and personal finances, Wilkes looked shrewdly to his future. Whenever he was offered snuff, he declined with the quip: "No, thank you. I have no *small* vices."

In politics or in the drawing room, only the foolhardy invited his ripostes. To an elector who proclaimed that he would rather vote for the devil, Wilkes snapped, "And what if your friend is not standing?"

One day a rival jeeringly informed him that "one of your supporters has turned his coat." "Impossible!" rejoined Wilkes. "Not one has a coat to turn."

Cynical, obscene, the idol of the mob though never the idol of the people, Wilkes was relentless when attacking. He took on anyone, regardless of reputation or field. He read with elation in Samuel Johnson's dictionary that "the letter H seldom, perhaps never, begins any but the first syllable." Wilkes immediately published a commentary that began:

"The author of this remark must be a man of quick appre-hension and compre-hensive genius; but I can never forgive his un-handsome be-haviour to the poor knight-hood, priest-hood and widow-hood, nor in-humanity to all man-hood."

Although he sat in the House of Commons, Wilkes had contempt for Parliament. An independent radical, he fought for the rights of the individual and for the reduction of the King's power. If he frequently voted with the Whig (Opposition) party, it was simply because the opinions of the Whigs coincided with his own on a given issue. They resented him almost as heartily as did the Tory government, though with a difference. The Whigs disliked him in the political arena only; the King and his ministers detested him under any roof.

Men were either for or against John Wilkes—violently. Samuel Martin, a dispenser of government bribes, practiced for a year with a pistol. Once confident of his skill, he goaded Wilkes into a duel, tricked him out of the choice of weapons, and wounded him severely.

Wilkes flayed the government through his paper, the *North Briton*. The famous issue of April 23, 1763, the forty-fifth, denounced His Majesty's speech before Parliament. In reprisal Wilkes was briefly imprisoned in the Tower of London. He was to be expelled four times from Parliament, fined, exiled, and outlawed.

His fame as a fighter for liberty spread to American shores. The Sons of Liberty wrote him often, pleading that he attach their grievances to his own in the House of Commons. When muskets sounded on one side of the Atlantic, on the other side John Wilkes poured out antiwar speeches with a sharpshooter's accuracy.

"What have we conquered?" he demanded in Commons after Bunker Hill. "Are we to pay as dearly for the rest of America?"

He told Parliament four months later: "I speak as a firm friend of England and America, but still more to universal liberty and rights of all mankind. I trust no part of the subjects of this vast empire will ever submit to be slaves."

As unofficial spokesman of the colonial cause in Parliament, Wilkes delivered ten prepared speeches. His words echoed in America from the patriot pages of the Boston *Gazette*.

The Whigs had decried the harsh measures that eventuated in the Revolution. Yet even Whig giants like Pitt and Edmund Burke scrupled at the idea of an independent America. When news of the Declaration of Independence reached England, the country had rallied to the King's war policy.

Before anyone else, Wilkes acknowledged that the Declaration of Independence made the colonies free. Ugly, squinting, rabble-rousing Wilkes stood almost alone. When another member of Parliament denounced Jefferson's document as ill-written and composed only with an eye to captivating the people, Wilkes thundered back: "The people are to decide this great controversy. If they are captivated by it, the end is attained."

It is the tragedy of history that words never settled a war, and words were all that Wilkes had to give. The Tories aided the British on the firing line. Wilkes could merely lend the rebels comfort. That he spoke against the war when most Englishmen favored it must be put down as an illustrious victory of honesty and courage.

The Gordon Riots of 1782, during which Wilkes, as Lord Mayor of London, jailed many of his supporters, cost him his popularity. Shortly afterward he retired and lived out the remaining seventeen years of his life, "an extinct volcano."

Licentious in private, courageous in public, lonely, and despite his howling followers, alone, John Wilkes kicked down many walls of despotism in England. He secured the abolition of general warrants, helped liberate the press, fought religious persecution, pioneered electioneering, and fearlessly championed the American cause.

Toward the close he cooled to the point of attending the King's levees. And to an old lady who shouted at him, "Wilkes and Liberty!" he gruffly reproved: "Be quiet, you old fool. That's all over long ago."

Nonetheless, some embers still smoldered. During a dinner attended by the dissolute Prince of Wales, a die-hard foe of Wilkes, the Prince asked for toasts. Wilkes proposed: "To the King—long may he live!"

Furious, the Prince, who despised his father, demanded to know when Wilkes had become so concerned over his parent's health.

"Since making the acquaintance of your Royal Highness," replied Wilkes, bowing low.

ARTEMAS WARD
First Commander in Chief

THE HUBBUB IN THE STREET DREW NEARER.

Judge Artemas Ward dragged himself from his sickbed to the window. People were hurrying toward his seven-room frame house, where a dust-coated express rider had pulled up to the gate.

At the sight of the judge, the rider cupped a lean brown hand to his mouth and called up the news. Then he whipped his foaming horse and raced out of Shrewsbury, trailing the echo of Lexington and Concord.

Aching Judge Ward sat down with a wince. Each stabbing attack of bladder stone was worse than the last. Suddenly there was this news to worry about as well. Some hothead had pulled a trigger. It looked as though the colony of Massachusetts had taken on the British Empire.

A muggy realization crept over Judge Ward, smothering his physical pains. He was the highest-ranking officer in Massachusetts. It was up to him to put right—one way or another—what had begun at Lexington.

BORN: November 26, 1727, Shrewsbury, Mass.
DIED: October 28, 1800, Shrewsbury, Mass.

He had never considered himself a military man. A Harvard graduate, he had started as a schoolteacher, shortly afterward abandoning teaching in favor of business, for he had a bride to support. In a lean-to behind his farmhouse he had established a general store.

For seven years he had sold everything from dry goods to rum. Gradually his interest in civic affairs had led him into public life full-time. He had climbed rapidly through the Shrewsbury township offices—tax assessor, clerk, moderator, treasurer, justice of the peace, and finally justice of the Worcester County Court.

If he did not fly to the army camps, nobody could blame him. His reputation was secure, his patriotism proved. For years he had championed colonial rights, toiling at the groundwork of conventions and at the First and Second Provincial Congresses.

The hour for action had struck, and it tolled over a county judge past his prime. He was forty-seven, sickly, and overweight.

Still, there was the uniform, *his* uniform, in the closet. It was that of a colonel of provincial militia, a seventeen-year-old relic of his months in the French and Indian War.

His uniform and his colony . . .

At dawn, Judge Artemas Ward, general of Massachusetts militia by vote of the Provincial Congress, squeezed and squirmed and tugged until he had all the buttons of his uniform fastened. He kissed his wife and eight children good-by. Mounting painfully, he rode toward Cambridge at the head of a company of minutemen neighbors.

On the way eastward, other militia units fell in with the Shrewsbury contingent. Closer to Boston, carriages and wagons appeared.

The carriages, crowded with wealthy Tory families and their possessions, were racing for the safety of Boston. Coming the opposite way were mostly wagons jammed with

women, children, and old men. They were the families of
the patriots departing the British stronghold for the surrounding villages.

A dreamlike air clung to the masses of men. Spanking
sunlight flashed off their bobbing squirrel guns, fowling
pieces, shovels, and axes. Something deep and strong as
freedom was going down the road with the sinewy farmers
and stout bakers and thick-armed smiths.

Arriving at Cambridge in the afternoon, Ward took
over command from William Heath, a fellow Massachusetts general but the judge's junior in order of appointment.
A thirty-eight-year-old farmer, Heath had borne the
fortunes of the rebels on his beefy shoulders through the
first day.

Into the area swarmed militia from Connecticut, Rhode
Island, and New Hampshire. Their leaders accepted Ward
as chief, at least for the moment. In a manner of speaking,
Massachusetts was the host colony. Here was the hotbed of
disloyalty, the battlefield, and the enemy.

Ward promptly set up headquarters in the white clap-
board house of Jonathan Hastings. He shed his tight uniform with relief. He donned a powdered wig, a long waistcoat, ruffled shirt and neckcloth, knee breeches, riding
boots, and finally a long coat with silver buttons.

He looked more like a civilian than a soldier. If he also
thought as a civilian, he was not without useful abilities.
He was slow but dependable and cautious. He considered
a Massachusetts man God's chosen creature, a winning
sentiment among the predominately local troops.

For this early watch-and-wait stage of the war, he may
well have been the ideal commander. An imaginative
general might have courted disaster by attacking. The
mobs of armed civilians could not maneuver, but they
might stand and defend.

Ward saw his job in terms of paper work—maps and

political protests. He had to bottle up the British regulars in Boston. The London government might tire of a siege and heed the grievances of the colonies. Then everyone could have an evening dram and go home.

Among his first acts was the calling of a council of war. Two generals, Heath and John Whitcomb, attended, along with six colonels and five lieutenant colonels. Decisions were reached on guard posts, troop deployments, fortifications, supply, and recruiting.

Ward directed himself to three tasks. He prepared for the British attempt to break out of Boston; he foresaw the need for more troops; and he tried to discipline the patriots into an army.

Almost immediately he was staggered by an unforeseen danger. The men deserted in droves. They had leaped to arms instinctively. Now they sat around idly brooding on their sick wives, their children, their crops. As Ward watched horrified, his army began strolling away.

Four days after Lexington he wrote the Massachusetts Provincial Congress: "If I have not enlisting orders immediately, I shall be left alone. It is impossible to keep the men here, excepting something is done."

The Congress appealed to the neighboring colonies of New England. By the end of May, about fifteen thousand citizen-soldiers swelled Ward's command. He had been, in the meantime, officially named Commander in Chief of the Massachusetts forces. The other troops continued to pay him voluntary obedience.

Frequently in such pain that he had to grit his teeth, the "judge" ran the Grand American Army (the newspapers' term) from his "courtroom" in the Hastings House in Cambridge. His two-man staff consisted of a cousin, Joseph Ward, as secretary, and Samuel Osgood as personal aide.

When the Battle of Bunker Hill was fought in Boston,

Ward was absent from the field in Cambridge. Technically, he had been replaced. Two days before, on June 15, 1775, the rich Colonel George Washington had been elected by the Continental Congress to command the armies. Corpulent Artemas Ward, passed over because of ill health, was elected "first major-general" and second-in-command.

Washington formally relieved him on July 3. Between the towering plantation owner in his gorgeous uniform and the sick, pudgy judge in his waistcoat, little love was spilled. Washington thought Ward had kept a flabby grip on matters. Ward turned purple over the aristocratic Virginian's opinion of his beloved Massachusetts men— "exceedingly dirty and nasty people."

Washington eased Ward into the background. When both armies moved to New York, Ward was left behind in the empty command of the defenses of Boston, because, as Washington remarked, Ward did not care to forsake "his own chimney smoke."

Thereafter Ward sought to retire from the military side of the conflict. Eventually Congress accepted his resignation, and on March 20, 1777, he gladly turned over his garrison to Heath. Henceforth he gave himself unstintingly to duties that better fitted his talents—to the Continental Congress, the Massachusetts legislature, and to numerous watchdog committees.

Never a man of destiny, Ward became a man without a face. His long sharp nose and pointed chin were eclipsed by the prominent features of George Washington in the American firmament.

Yet Ward had not messed the job. He accomplished nearly all that was asked of him in those shaky first days. Although critically short of artillery, he stopped up the British regulars in Boston.

If the name Artemas Ward is mentioned today, the man probably referred to is Artemus Ward, the pseudonym of humorist Charles Farrar Brown, who lived in the next century. The Artemas Ward who commanded the American forces for seventy-five days with such colorless adequacy could not even attract a biographer.

In 1921 the first full-length story of his life appeared at last. The author was hired by Ward's great-great-grandson, who had to pay the printer to publish the manuscript.

ISRAEL PUTNAM
Old Put

THE YOUNG FARMER WAS A NEWCOMER TO POMFRET, CON-
necticut. He was not a member of the church, the school
committee, or the library association. He could barely
write, and he frequently stuttered. He had, nevertheless,
the likable frankness of a man making his own way. And he
alone in the village volunteered to crawl in after the wolf.

During the winter of 1742–1743 the wolf had preyed
upon the countryside. She had been tracked to a rock-
bound passage tunneling into a cave, where all efforts to
dislodge her had failed. Straw and brimstone had been
burned in the mouth of the passageway. Hounds had been
shooed in only to limp back yelping and bleeding. The
wolf had to be taken soon, before sundown. During the
night she might escape by another outlet.

The young farmer fastened a rope about his waist.
Holding a blazing torch, he inched down into the cold
"mansion of horror." At the far end he saw the wolf's

BORN: January 7, 1718, Salem, Mass.
DIED: May 29, 1790, Pomfret, Conn.

glaring eyeballs. He returned to the surface, got his pistol, and worked down again. One shot, fired as the wolf hunched to spring, ended the scourge of Pomfret's livestock.

The one shot did more than stop a sheep killer. It showered attention upon the rough, half-schooled farmer, Israel Putnam. Even more important, it dramatized Putnam's self-confidence and bravery.

For it was this same self-confidence and bravery during the Revolution thirty-two years later that impelled "Old Put" to accept topflight commands. Unfortunately the care and conduct of an army requires special training and talent besides, and he possessed neither.

He was to ride off to the Revolution not without combat experience. At the outbreak of the French and Indian War in 1756 he raised the first company in Connecticut. As its captain he marched away, leaving his prosperous farm in the keeping of his oldest son.

Putnam thirsted for action and found it with Major Robert Rogers. The first time the two men ventured on a mission together, Captain Putnam saved the life of the famed guerrilla. The following year Putnam narrowly missed being burned at the stake by Indians.

One memorable day a British officer challenged him to a fight. Having the choice of weapons, Putnam selected a keg of powder, upon which both men sat while a flame was applied to a long fuse. The Redcoat kept his seat until the flame licked close. Then he leaped up and ran for dear life. Putnam bruised his ribs laughing. The keg contained onions lightly sprinkled with a few grains of powder.

After he had served throughout the entire French and Indian War, Putnam soldiered another year against Pontiac, the Indian Chief. Discharged a lieutenant colonel, he resumed the life of a wealthy farmer. He accepted a leading part in local patriotic groups as opposition to the King took adamant shape.

In 1774, Pomfret made a gift of sheep to the hungry people of Boston, who were feeling the pinch of British disfavor. In his dual role as town officer and farmer, Putnam shepherded the flock on the long trip to the city. The heavily charged anti-British emotions registered on him sharply. The showdown was very near.

When it happened, he was in the fields. A son, Daniel, sixteen, witnessed his father's headlong reaction to the news that the dispatch rider brought of Lexington and Concord.

"He loitered not," wrote Daniel, "but left me, the driver of his team, to unyoke it in the furrow, and not many days later to follow him to camp."

Putnam whipped off his leather apron, threw a saddle on an old white farm horse, and started for Cambridge. On the way he summoned the militia officers of every town through which he traveled. He arrived in Cambridge on April 21, having ridden the same horse practically nonstop for ninety miles.

Artemas Ward assigned Putnam, a brigadier general of Connecticut militia, to the command of the crucial center sector. By May the spirited old farmer was arguing to fortify the Charlestown Peninsula. Ward overruled him. Such an action, Ward feared, might ignite a general engagement. For that, the Americans were woefully unprepared.

Several weeks later the Americans learned that the British planned to occupy Dorchester Heights on June 18. The Heights menaced Boston from the south as Charlestown menaced the city from the north.

To counter the British move, American units marched up Bunker Hill at the northern end of the peninsula at sunset on June 16. Putnam conferred with Colonel Richard Gridley, the chief engineer. Putnam listened attentively and then did exactly as he pleased. He ordered the soldiers off Bunker Hill and onto a smaller, less defensible hill a half mile to the south, Breed's Hill.

Old Put had come to fight. He didn't see much point in the British sitting behind impregnable positions on Dorchester Heights while the Americans did the same thing on Bunker Hill.

Breed's Hill excited the old warrior for two reasons. First, it rose within cannon-shot of Boston and therefore its capture would alarm the British. Second, its sides fell in tempting, gentle slopes that seemed agreeable to an infantry assault . . .

Having marked out the stage, Putnam the farmer picked up a shovel and showed what must be done. By morning the works on Breed's Hill were nearly completed. By afternoon, the British, eschewing a thrust to the rear, rose to the attack.

The battle descends to us as the Battle of Bunker Hill, a misnomer. Fought on Breed's Hill, it developed into the fiercest, costliest battle of the entire war. Putnam was everywhere nerving up his men. Garbed in a checkered shirt and astride his ancient white nag, he looked the picture of "a yeoman warrior, fresh from the plow."

"Wait till you see the whites of their eyes," he ordered.

In the thick of the fray he spied an old friend, British Major John Small, suddenly exposed to fire. "For God's sake," shouted Putnam to his men. "Spare that man! I love him as a brother!" Another old friend on the British side, Lieutenant Colonel James Abercromby, fell mortally wounded. Carried to a boat, Abercromby called out: "If you catch Old Put, don't hang him. He's a good soldier."

The British swept up. Two magnificent waves shattered upon American flintlocks. The Redcoats gallantly mustered a third. Deprived of reinforcements, low on ammunition, the Americans stared at the bayonets, broke, and fled.

Eventually white-haired Putnam steadied them. On

Prospect Hill on the mainland, a mile from Charlestown Neck, he directed new entrenchments, placing sod with his own hands.

Just who commanded the rebels at Bunker Hill is uncertain. Colonel William Prescott led at the front lines. Prescott, however, failed to win promotion during the rest of the Revolution, and his true abilities seemed gilded by the heroism of his men.

Putnam apparently exercised overall control, managing the battle without a single aide to bring or carry reports. Two days later he received his commission as major general, ranking in order of appointment only behind Ward, Lee, and Schuyler, and the only one of the four to be elected unanimously by the Congress. The vote testifies to his popularity rather than to his prowess as a general officer.

After the British evacuated Boston, Putnam was ordered to New York. For ten days before Washington's arrival, he held the chief command, and blame for the fiasco on Long Island falls upon his head.

Several German officers, prisoners of the Battle of Trenton, visited him in Philadelphia on New Year's Day, 1777. "He shook hands with each of us," one German wrote in his journal, "and we all had a glass of Madeira with him. This old graybeard may be a good honest man, but nobody but the rebels would have made him a general."

After overseeing the removal of stores and troops from New York, the old graybeard began to drop in Washington's esteem. His posts were farther and farther from the fighting: command of the Hudson Highlands in 1777, recruiting and garrison duty in Connecticut in 1778–1779, and then section commander on the Hudson in 1779.

That same year a stroke paralyzed his right arm and forced his retirement.

His shortcomings and failures may be in part, at least,

traced to the focus of history, which fixed upon him in the wrong war. By the Battle of Bunker Hill he was fifty-seven. The lightning brilliance of Rogers' Rangers is lost in the sunburst of change that was the Revolution.

By 1775, Old Put was outdated in all things but love of country and the will to fight.

WILLIAM HOWE
General Reluctant

HIS SWARTHY FACE STREAKED WITH SWEAT AND POWDER, his regimentals smeared with the blood of his soldiers, General William Howe gazed in baffled disbelief toward Breed's Hill.

The Americans still held the slope. By all the rules of war, they should have thrown down their muskets and run clear back to their pigs and plows. Yet twice they had risen up to repulse his scarlet regulars. Behind an overnight fort of breastworks and a redoubt, they were defying the British Empire.

The puny hill and the jack-in-the-box defense lent the afternoon a toylike distortion. Distance shrank the background to miniature size. On Howe's left, the village of Charlestown burned like a bundle of twigs under the bombardment of British men-of-war. Across the Charles River, the wee rooftops of Boston were sprinkled with the dots of people crowding to witness death and dying.

BORN: August 10, 1729
DIED: July 12, 1814, Plymouth, England

Howe's fellow generals, Clinton and Burgoyne, who had arrived with him last month, were over there. Watching with them on Copp's Hill was outworn General Gage. Although Gage retained nominal command, the battle was Howe's to direct—a job for which he had little heart. His political sympathies and the memory of his brother softened his feelings toward the enemy.

One good licking, he had thought. Give the Americans a whopping lesson to show them how futile it was to believe they could win their freedom by dint of arms! He had scorned as a trick Clinton's idea of slipping behind the enemy. A frontal assault . . .

Somebody handed him a goblet of wine. No, not his valet Evans. A ball in the arm had sent poor Evans staggering back to the boats with the maimed battalions.

Howe rubbed dirt from his lips with a dark hand and drank. Once more his eyes lifted to the incredible rebels. He cursed the English law that required every colonist to own a gun in order to defend the King's government.

A light gust suddenly cleared the haze of smoke and dust. The sun blazed down mercilessly upon the red-coated bodies strewn everywhere—on the rail fence, near the ditch, and in the tall grass beyond. The bravest lay like bright discarded dolls, a bayonet lunge from the enemy.

Turning from the hill, Howe saw reinforcements being rowed slowly toward Morton's Point. It would take about twenty minutes for them to reach his position, and thirty minutes for the two batteries, already under way, to buck the tide and come up to sweep the Americans. He dared not wait. The foe was massing on Bunker Hill to the rear. Before they made up their minds to join the battle, Howe knew he must try it again.

In eighteen years of soldiering, William Howe had never before experienced fear. Suddenly doubt and dread charged "a moment I never felt before." He steadied his voice.

"Drop your packs, gentlemen. Once more we will go forward."

Soldiers who had twice survived the blood-wet slope gratefully sloughed equipment that weighed a hundred pounds. Howe did not object when many shed their great-coats too. In their shirt-sleeves they looked oddly like the enemy.

He signaled. The drums beat and the beat quickened. Although believing they must again charge a foe who outnumbered them three to one, the exhausted men shuffled forward over their dead. It was to be—in the words of a British army historian—"one of the greatest feats of arms ever credited" to British soldiery.

Take nothing from these nameless, forgotten English-men, these marvels of obedience and valor. But on this third assault Howe saw once more their inadequate training (so different were they from the scaling party of twenty-four veterans he had led up the Heights of Abraham to spear-head Wolfe's victory fifteen years before!). The men in the rear, aiming uphill at the rebels, fired into the backs of their comrades ahead of them.

Howe brandished his sword and screamed to his officers. "Go to the bayonets, gentlemen! *The bayonets!*"

The muskets leveled. "Conquer or die!" sergeants yelled. The hoarsely panting men crouched and thrust. Before the glint of horrible pain, the enemy panicked. Abruptly the redoubt was clear. The British Empire had been yanked from the abyss of humiliation by that maligned breed of mankind, the professional foot soldier.

Clinton, having crossed from Boston, urged Howe to pursue the disorganized rebels. Howe shook his head. The cost of one hill had been more than a thousand men, a third of his force. He ordered the heights fortified.

The Battle of Bunker Hill, the first and perhaps the bloodiest battle of the Revolution, ended as the clink of entrenching tools sounded through the warm twilight of June 17, 1775. On the mainland, the Americans were to recover quickly, buoyed by the knowledge that they had stood off British regulars. But for want of powder or reinforcements, they might have held Breed's Hill.

Shortly past five o'clock, Howe stepped wearily into a boat and was rowed back to Boston. What swirled in his mind? Certainly he did not think of the bath and clean uniform ahead.

His thoughts become manifest by his subsequent actions. Having stood among his slaughtered men, Howe never again ordered an assault if the rebels were entrenched behind even the thinnest of barricades.

Howe's strange conduct of the war, however, answered to other influences besides Bunker Hill. Time after time during his two years as Commander in Chief, he let canny Washington slip away, or he withheld pursuit after a shattering victory. To Alexander Hamilton such unaccountable bungling, often at the brink of total victory, made Howe an "unintelligible fellow."

At the core of the mystery was Howe's dearth of enthusiasm for service against the colonies. The grateful people of Massachusetts had placed a monument in Westminster Abbey to honor his brother, George Augustus, who had fallen at Ticonderoga in the war against the French and Indians. A Whig member of Parliament, Howe had promised his constituents that he would never take up the sword against the colonists. He had broken the promise in order to "serve my country in distress" when an American command had been *ordered*, not offered, him by his second cousin, the King.

Howe the Whig member of Parliament shackled Howe the general. Almost to the close of his tenure in America he and his brother, Admiral Richard Howe, made peace overtures. They hoped against hope after each defeat that the chastened enemy would hungrily clutch the chance to live in peace as royal subjects again.

Three months after Bunker Hill, Howe formally took the top command from Gage. Fighting with a sword in one hand and an olive branch in the other, he diligently refrained from bagging the foe. The record of his battles sing of his unwillingness to strike the final blow.

At Brooklyn Heights (for which he was knighted), Harlem, and White Plains he allowed the rebels to retreat unhampered. He stopped Cornwallis' pursuit at Brunswick. He delayed at Princeton and Brandywine.

After each victory he seemed to have "calculated with accuracy the exact time necessary for his enemy to escape." The Tories bitterly assailed him as a traitor. Israel Putnam, who commanded against him at Bunker Hill, called him either a "friend of America or no general."

Putnam erred in his second surmise. William Howe stood every inch a general. With his large fleet and splendid army, he outmaneuvered Washington whenever he chose to come to grips.

The victory at Brandywine permitted Howe to seize Philadelphia, the enemy capital. It was a blunder. General Burgoyne was then driving down the Hudson Valley from Canada. Had Howe gone up the river and joined Burgoyne, Schuyler's rebel army might have been trapped. Instead he turned to Philadelphia and abandoned Burgoyne to his doom at Saratoga.

By then, October, 1777, Howe realized his self-appointed role as "Great Conciliator to the Colonies" was a hollow dream. He sent his letter of resignation to London.

While awaiting a reply, Sir Billy gave himself to "his glass, his lass, and his game of cards." He did nothing about the Americans withering away at Valley Forge. Their plight, he asserted, "did not justify an attack on that strong position during the severe winter."

His resignation was accepted. On May 24, 1778, he sailed off to face a Parliamentary inquiry. Had the inquiry been pressed to a finish, he doubtlessly would have been cashiered.

William Howe's Revolutionary career is a muted war song. By stifling the bugles of pursuit, he had fought to win a peace, not a war.

HENRY CLINTON

Portrait in the Background

THE WATCH ABOARD H.M.S. *Lively* HEARD IT FIRST.

Over the darkened Charles River sounded the ring of pickaxes glancing off hidden rocks.

The Americans were fortifying night-shrouded Breed's Hill on the Charlestown Peninsula some one hundred yards off the bow of the British warship. Captain Bishop bawled the order to open fire. Broadside after broadside slashed from hull and deck.

Other British warships in the harbor quickly added their salvos. Across the river in Boston, sentries relayed the news that the Americans were busy entrenching. Henry Clinton, a chubby, fair-haired man of thirty-seven, hurried to the three-story Province House to alert the Commander in Chief, Thomas Gage. They were soon joined by five tense men including William Howe and John Burgoyne.

Clinton, Howe, and Burgoyne, major generals all, had been sent by the King to reinforce the beleaguered Gage.

BORN: 1738 (?), Newfoundland (?)
DIED: December 23, 1795, Gibraltar

Arriving in Boston three weeks ago, the trio had learned to their astonishment that hostilities had already begun.

Howe had worked out a plan to destroy the rebels if they foolishly persisted in armed protest. He intended to fight the day after tomorrow. But somebody—was it Burgoyne? —had talked, and the brash rebels had seized the Charlestown heights first.

Around the walnut council table that night the faces were grim and the hearts more nearly faint than stout. None wanted to light the fuse of the struggle that would flare up beyond their wildest dreams.

Gage had an American wife, deep ties with the New World, and the forlorn hope that a large proportion of Massachusetts was loyal to the Crown. Howe held a low opinion of Gage and a high regard for the Americans, who had honored his brother. Burgoyne had contended in England that conciliation was the better part of militarism. Clinton had been raised in New York while his father was governor, and he had pleasant childhood memories to pit against a soldier's sense of duty.

Of the four, shy Henry Clinton voiced the soundest answer to the rebel army. The first stroke against it, he insisted, must be "important and certain of success." He urged an all-out attack at daybreak before the preparations on Breed's Hill reached completion.

His proposal was an extension of the punitive frontal assault planned by Howe. While Howe attacked from the tip of the Charlestown Peninsula, Clinton's scheme had himself leading five hundred men up the Mystic River and landing behind the Americans to block their retreat.

Such a thrust, Clinton admitted, would expose him to the fire of the great swarm of rebels on the mainland. But, he argued, he had the protection of the British ships, galleys, gunboats, and other water batteries.

He was overruled. The cautious Gage felt the risk of

landing between the two parts of the enemy—each part larger than Clinton's expedition—violated sound military principles. Besides, Gage doubted that he had enough flat-bottom craft to transport both Howe's regiments and Clinton's encircling commandos.

So Howe's plan—an unadorned frontal assault—stood as conceived. Had he put it into action when Clinton urged—at daybreak of June 17, 1775, *before* the rebel entrenchments were advanced—the Redcoats might have easily overrun the heights. Not until afternoon did the careful Howe get his men, stooped under an overload of equipment, landed in two contingents on the peninsula.

Clinton watched with Burgoyne from Copp's Hill in Boston. The city had become a vast stadium. On the field of Charlestown "the most dramatic spectator event in history" boiled and smoked toward a climax as the rebels twice repulsed stirring British charges.

Clinton drummed his spyglass against his palm. Although assigned to forward reinforcements upon Howe's call, he decided he could be more useful on the field. He told Burgoyne to apologize to General Gage for exceeding his orders. Then, with paunch jiggling at every step, he hurried toward the water.

As his boat put into Charlestown, bullets singed his hat and wounded two of his oarsmen. He jumped ashore, surveyed the carnage, and scribbled a report to Gage.

Once his hands were again free for sword and pistol, he collected all the disheartened guards and wounded men who would follow him, "which to their honor were many," and led them toward the firing.

By marching his bandaged brigade smartly, Clinton hoped to create the illusion of newly arrived units. The ruse succeeded. He saved the British left and restored order to the confused, exhausted troops just after they had swept over Breed's Hill.

Puffing up to the white-faced Howe, Clinton wrung permission to lead a follow-up charge against Bunker Hill, where the rebel Putnam was exerting himself to salvage the day. Howe consented and again Clinton succeeded.

With the rebels beaten back across Charlestown Neck, Clinton pleaded for the chance to pursue with light troops. *Now* was the fleeting moment to quash the uprising for good.

Howe gripped his elbow fiercely. Enough blood had been spilled for one day.

So Henry Clinton, a short-winded, unlikely looking hero, returned to Boston, where Gage had instructed him to stay. Although covered with Howe's highest praises and flushed with victory, he harbored two baleful misgivings.

He worried that "a few such victories" as Bunker Hill "would shortly put an end to British dominion in America." And he worried that his success could not justify his disobedience.

Opposing drives—wanting success and fearing it, self-doubt and daring—were among the tensions tugging at Henry Clinton. As battle piled upon battle, his inner discords transformed him into the most fascinating acrobat in uniform. While standing in the foreground of events, he managed to remain obscurely in the background. When he replaced Howe as Commander in Chief in May, 1778, his self-conflicts merged with the incompetence of the Ministry. The effect was to hobble Britain's war effort and eventually to paralyze it.

Bunker Hill is a microcosm of so much of his career. There he first evinced his love of envelopment: while his encircling movement of Breed's Hill from the Mystic River was rejected, he later planned the epic envelopment of Long Island. There he first gave advice to his superiors (Gage and Howe) with a freedom that verged on defiance, and so with few exceptions, notably Long Island, his counsels were seldom heeded. There he disregarded Gage's orders to remain in Boston and thus hinted at the coming friction in his relations with his superiors and equals, especially in the navy. He soon fell out with Howe, even as Cornwallis, his own second-in-command later on, was to fall out with him.

While Clinton was under Gage and then Howe, his plans and actions were colored by daring. When he assumed the grand responsibility of Commander in Chief, audacity paled into indecision. He vacillated even about resigning. It was as if he hungered for authority and then declined to use it forcefully out of dread of failure. The prospect of losing all his troops, as had nearly occurred at Bunker Hill, hounded him.

In his seven years in America (four as Commander in Chief), Henry Clinton participated in surprisingly few engagements. His fame as a subordinate rests firmly on his vital roles at Bunker Hill and Long Island, and on the capture of the Hudson River forts. As Commander in Chief, his reputation hinges on one fray, Monmouth, and on one siege, Charleston.

He was a man of contradictions even to his battles: the foremost pair stand at opposite poles. At Charleston in May of 1780, he was the hero who inflicted upon the Americans their worst disaster till Bataan in 1942. By his indecision during the Virginia campaign in 1781, he shares the blame for Yorktown, the worst British disaster till Dunkirk in 1940.

Clinton turned over his office to Sir Guy Carleton after the fall of Yorktown. He had held a top command longer than anyone in either army except Washington. He sailed for home and the unprized rank of scapegoat.

The year before his death he was made governor of Gibraltar. Shelved, forgotten, frustrated, he brightened the lonely hours by grinding a high polish into an account of his Revolutionary campaigns.

He hoped the work, the labor of the last twelve years of

his life, would redeem his honor. In its pages he nudged all
responsibility for failure onto others, particularly Cornwallis, who was traveling a course strewn with fresh laurels.

He was done out of his revenge, even as he neurotically
contrived to do himself out of glory, by dying before the
manuscript was ready for the printer. It was not published
until 1954.

HENRY KNOX

Father of the Artillery Corps

HENRY KNOX HEARD HIS NAME CALLED BEFORE HE WAS near enough to distinguish either of the riders jogging toward him. After another hundred yards had been closed, he recognized both men, and immediately spurred toward them at a gallop.

The skinny rider slouching like an India ink sketch of Don Quixote was General Charles Lee. The other officer Knox had never seen close up. Yet an instant's scrutiny of the erect figure in the immaculate blue-and-buff uniform sufficed to confirm all Knox had heard. It was the tall, perfectly poised Virginian whom the Congress had sent up four days ago to be Commander in Chief.

General Washington had ridden out with Lee to inspect parts of the rebel siege lines rising crudely around British-held Boston. At Lee's request, Knox turned back and conducted the generals about the fortifications he had helped to lay out at Roxbury on the right wing.

Four days after the tour, which took place on July 5,

BORN: July 25, 1750, Boston, Mass.
DIED: October 25, 1806, Thomaston, Maine

1775, Knox told his brother, "General Washington fills his place with ease and dignity."

Washington was equally impressed. He regarded the quadrangular Roxbury Fort as the best planned of all the works under construction. And he marked well the huge young volunteer who talked like a professor of tactics and covered ground with a springy gait for all his two hundred and fifty pounds. In an army officered by horse traders, apothecaries, tanners, hatters, and whatnots, a man of such superior military training was a rare find.

Afterward, Washington learned the astonishing truth. The twenty-five-year-old Knox was a Boston bookdealer with a varnish of militia training. To accommodate the British officers who patronized his shop, Knox had stocked military manuals, and he had devoted all his leisure to studying their pages.

For the next four months Knox continued building fortifications. On November 17, Washington put him in charge of army artillery, though Knox had never fired a cannon in battle, and recommended him for a colonel's commission.

Knox probably wondered what he was to command. The patriots had a few light cannon, most of them looted from ships or brought in by New Hampshire men. Small of caliber, they could neither support an infantry assault nor answer British siege cannon.

Fortunately the American shortage was balanced by British caution, producing a stalemate in the last half of 1775. Still, the rebels knew what to expect. New armies, combat-strengthened by German mercenaries, would soon be crossing the Atlantic to crush the insurrection.

The Americans had one source of artillery—Fort Ticonderoga, captured six months earlier by Ethan Allen. More than one hundred and twenty guns gaped silently from its masonry walls. The problem was how to fetch them over nearly three hundred miles of rivers, mountains, and choking forest with winter approaching.

Knox viewed the problem with an optimistic eye. Winter came as a friend. Ice transformed waterways into highways. Snow filled ruts and slickened jarring mountain trails.

Washington listened and told the enthusiastic Knox to make the attempt. The former shopkeeper rode forty miles a day and reached Fort Ticonderoga on the evening of December 5.

The venerable stronghold reared amid the mighty, natural splendor of fir and pine slopes. Below, Lake Champlain stretched in serene majesty, accentuating the grandeur of nature and the immensity of the human task. Knox was undismayed. He was accustomed to doing things on his own.

Since his father had disappeared in the West Indies when he was nine, he had worked to support his mother and younger brother. He had married Lucy Flucker over the objections of her Tory parents. The jolly, robust girl was never far from his thoughts. And though she was to grow "frighteningly" large, she stayed light enough afoot to be Washington's favorite dancing partner.

At Ticonderoga the only music was the undanceable melodies of the winds that howled off the bastions while Henry Knox, volunteer artilleryman, sorted the guns. Many of them were dangerously corroded. He found fifty-nine usable pieces ranging from 4-pounders to 24-pounders. For the high-angle firing necessary to throw shells over earthworks, he took four howitzers and some mortars ranging from small cohorns to a trio of hefty 13-inchers.

Leaving sufficient arms for the defense of the fort, Knox marshaled his mixed workgang of soldiers and civilians and loaded his vital cargo onto stoneboats and block carriages. Along with the artillery, he took away a barrel of flints, and twenty-three boxes of lead.

Now commenced a forty-seven-day trek of clogging snow and frustrating thaws, of numbed hands and feet and cracking whips, of sliding, heaving, hauling, and cursing.

From the outset Knox showed himself a resourceful leader. With the foresight, friendliness, and ebullient spirits that were to stamp him in the heartbreaking days to come, with daring and ingenuity, he drove his sixty-ton caravan toward Boston.

He fixed the weight each horse and ox must pull and kept himself posted on the daily progress of each driver. He developed an efficient system of spacing the sleds, and he solved every obstacle in his path. Once, upon reaching the Hudson, he discovered that the ice was treacherously thin. He ordered holes cut. Water gurgled up, flooding over the surface and freezing. Upon this double layer of ice the sleds passed safely across.

Throughout the ordeal he never spared himself, and he proved to be a sharp bargainer in the constant task of hiring fresh oxen and horses and sleds and teamsters. When the deep snow thwarted his horse, he dismounted and slogged ahead on foot. When his men threatened to mutiny because of the conditions, he talked to them for three hours since he could not *order* the soldiers among them to continue. He was a civilian pending the approval of his commission.

The men stuck with him and the local inhabitants wondered why. Everywhere the people turned out to marvel at the lumbering gun-train, the steaming animals, the straining men. Some said the Berkshire Hills could not be passed, there were no roads. Henry Knox made his own. Up and through he went, coming down with anchoring ropes lashed about successive trees to check the crazily swinging sleds.

Guns were lost. Sleds overturned and broke. Oxen and

horses died with their hooves balled in snow and their nostrils lined with ice.

But Henry Knox let no man quit, and he brought the artillery in.

Most of the cannon were mounted on the works guarding Cambridge. The heaviest pieces were rushed to Dorchester Heights on the extreme right. Washington breathed more easily as he waited for the next move of the besieged British.

The American army now packed an all-purpose wallop. Knox did not differentiate between field artillery, and that for garrison and coastal defense. He had his guns, and he applied himself to training his men to use them in support of the infantry.

Trenton, Princeton, and Monmouth received the devastating bombardments of Knox's artillerymen. They outdueled and smashed the British cannoneers at Yorktown and gave Knox his crowning reward for seven years of hope and dedication.

Lafayette was so excited by the American gunners at Yorktown that he declared them "one of the wonders of the Revolution." Knox may have smiled at the compliment, remembering a bitter day of humiliation back in 1776 when the British fleet had sailed disdainfully up the Hudson and East Rivers. His inexperienced gunners could do nothing—except to wound six of their own men.

As the years of war burned away, Washington grew ever closer to his good-humored, optimistic artillery chief. In matters of the big guns, he trusted him implicitly. Barring possibly Lafayette, Knox was closer to him than was any man. Washington loved him for his ability, his spirit, and even his voice. It was the great bass shouts of Henry Knox that had relayed Washington's orders above the wild night storm that Christmas night they crossed the Delaware to Trenton.

It was Knox who fought for a selective service system,

for one uniform, for unit flags, for a naval academy, and for a national militia. It was Knox who first called Washington "Father of His Country."

In 1785, Congress elected him Secretary of War. He participated in almost every important event during the formation of the United States till his retirement in 1796 to "Montepelier," his baronial estate in Maine.

Today nine counties, seventeen cities, and Fort Knox, the national gold depository, are named for the young bookseller who emerged like a miracle from his shop to organize, equip, and command the United States Army Artillery Corps.

GEORGE GERMAIN

My Poor Horses

LORD GEORGE SACKVILLE, THE HARD-RIDING COMMANDER of the English expeditionary force, peered at the battle smoke that darkened the German plain. The French foe was reeling toward Minden. His own cavalrymen, leaning forward in their saddles ready to charge, looked toward him expectantly.

Lord George kept riding hard.

Back and forth he rode, back and forth, a fine-looking general upon a fine, foaming stallion. He held the animal under perfect restraint: the flying hoofs never misstepped in the direction of the enemy.

On this blistering morning of August 1, 1759, Lord George galloped upon the summit of his military career. He had come to Germany as second-in-command to Charles Spencer in one of Pitt's buccaneering expeditions against the French. When Spencer had died in an epidemic in Münster ten months before, Sackville, a soldier for twenty-two years, had succeeded him.

BORN: June 26, 1716, Haymarket, England
DIED: August 26, 1785, Stoneland Lodge, England

Back and forth he rode till he was overtaken by an aide-de-camp of the Duke of Brunswick, the Commander in Chief. The aide barked at the confused Englishman. It was the Duke's order that he advance to the left with the right wing of his cavalry.

Lord George wheeled toward the battle. He watched a cannonball flick away the head of a horse. "I—I do not comprehend how the movement is to be made," he stammered.

The aide rode off in a fury. Lord George resumed his dexterous horsemanship. He ignored repeated orders from the Duke. He blinded himself to the contemptuous glances of his officers. For half an hour the English squadrons stayed put. The great moment slipped by, and the French escaped annihilation.

England welcomed the returning soldier like a shipload of smallpox. "He was universally deserted," wrote Lord Shelburne. "No one would speak to him in the Commons or anywhere else."

Lord George, a bullhead on a stiff neck, argued self-righteously that nothing could be justly alleged against him. He demanded a court-martial to refute the accusation of cowardice, and he got one. It found him forever "unfit to serve His Majesty in any Military capacity whatever."

The disgraced general bellowed that the court had not done him justice. History agrees with him. The sentence should have omitted the word "Military."

For in November, 1775, Lord George leaped out of the trapdoor of dishonor to succeed Lord Dartmouth as Secretary of State for the Colonies and hence for the Revolutionary War.

His leap, perhaps bewildering to the innocent bystander, was actually the final, crowning phase of a long uphill campaign during which he received two mighty boosts. First, King George II, who detested him, died a year after

Minden. Then Lady Betty Germain willed him her fortune, provided he change his name. He complied with stunning speed. Prudently, however, he retained his first name, given him in honor of George I, who had attended his christening as godfather.

He had wealth, a new name, and the thickest hide in Europe. Thus armored, he withstood the insults hurled from the floor of Parliament and the lampoons of pamphleteers and cartoonists. Kissing hands as Lord Germain, he started to worm his way out of the muck of Minden.

He attached himself body and soul to Lord Bute, tutor and first prime minister of the new king, George III. At every opportunity he clambered to identify himself as one of the King's friends. He loudly favored stern discipline for the colonies.

The guilt of his Cabinet appointment falls on the head of Lord Frederick North, the wartime prime minister. Germain's advance into the royal sun, his wiggling and his squirming, resembled action. His large size and his skill as a speaker sharpened the illusion until the grotesque miscasting resulted. To the easygoing Lord North, the man of action passed for the man of capability.

Within three months the new secretary repaid his benefactor by terming him a "trifling and supine Prime Minister."

The war was going badly for England when the horseman of Minden, presented with this second chance, clutched the reins. His years in office fill the gap between incompetence and catastrophe.

Like all the men around George III, he overestimated the military value of the American loyalists. Germain clung to his faith in the loyalists with more persistance than anyone, and nothing crippled British strategy more than his overestimation. As late as 1781 he was misinterpreting their strength. He saw in the easy movements of Generals

Cornwallis and Prevost through the south the "indubitable proof of the indisposition of the inhabitants to support the rebel government." He simply never understood the retreating tactics of Nathanael Greene.

The prospect of England's confirmed foe, France, entering the war alongside the Americans seemed farfetched to Germain. Before France signed the alliance in February, 1778, he predicted that "Doctor Franklin would not be able to procure any open assistance." When Spain joined France in May, 1779, Germain landed upon a nifty way out of England's mounting woes. Bribe General Washington and his Continental Army back to England by guaranteeing them the plunder of the Spanish possessions in the New World!

Germain burdened the navy as well as the army with his authority. On March 8, 1778, he instructed Clinton that if he was unable to goad Washington to a decisive battle he should prepare amphibious operations. Germain wanted "to attack the Ports on the Coast, from New York to Nova Scotia, and to seize or destroy every ship or vessel in the different Creeks or Harbors . . . and also to destroy all Wharfs and Stores and Materials for Shipbuilding so as to incapacitate them from raising a Marine, or continuing their Depredations upon the Trade of this Kingdom."

This grandiose policy of burning the seaports never got off the water; the necessary ships could not be spared. The French navy kept the strongest elements of the British navy busy patrolling home coasts.

Part of the shortage of ships in America may be attributed to Germain's other office—that of Commissioner of Trade and Plantations. Bowing to the powerful interests in London that demanded protection for the West Indian plantations, he stationed fleets in Jamaica and the Leeward Islands. Had he attached less importance to the West Indies, his admiral there, George Rodney, might have sent all his ships after French Admiral de Grasse instead of only fourteen. Outnumbered by the French in the naval phase of the Yorktown battle, the timid British fleet eventually sacrificed Cornwallis and lost the war.

Deaf to advice except where it profited him personally, unable to initiate workable plans, quick to seek refuge behind the King, meddlesome and given to intrigue, Germain for all this might have yet come out of the war no worse than other high office holders. But there was the monstrous episode of his cold horses.

The situation was this. Burgoyne was in Canada about to march south to unite at Albany with Howe, who was to drive north from New York. Success meant the isolation of New England.

The final dispatches to Burgoyne were completed when Germain stuck his head into his office. It was a chilly day, and he was in a hurry to spend a weekend at his country mansion, Stoneland Lodge, in Sussex.

The orders to Howe had not yet been fair copied, but it would take only a few minutes, Germain was assured by D'Oyly, a deputy secretary.

"My poor horses must stand in the street all the time, and I shan't be on my time anywhere," complained Germain. D'Oyly said it would be all right. He would write Howe and enclose copies of Burgoyne's orders. Germain departed happy.

D'Oyly forgot to write. Howe remained in New York while Burgoyne pushed south toward a phantom column, and the risen strength of the rebels fell upon him at Saratoga.

Six months before England recognized America's independence, Germain saw the handwriting on the wall. The King's friends were finished. He resigned and demanded his reward. He desired a title, for as younger son he was only a courtesy lord.

George III offered a baronage. No, as a baron, observed

Germain, he would be outranked by his secretary, his lawyer, and Sir Jeffery Amherst, his father's former page. The King agreed. Viscount Germain, then? Better—but Lady Betty Germain was long in her grave. He had her money and estates, and would it not be nice to have his own name again, too?

As Viscount Sackville he presented himself in the House of Lords. Many members of that august body howled in disgust. But tradition prevailed. The motion to bar him was defeated, as was the subsequent motion to oust him.

George Sackville, the man who had done more than any single individual to wreck Britain's first empire, settled in his seat, beaming.

EZEK HOPKINS

Amateur Admiral

SHORTLY AFTER NINE O'CLOCK OF A COLD WINTER MORNING a barge nudged awkwardly into the slip at the end of Walnut Street in Philadelphia. Ezek Hopkins, an elderly figure self-consciously wearing a gaudy new uniform, gingerly hopped aboard. The barge took him through the floating ice to the 440-ton *Alfred*.

The instant Hopkins stepped on deck, the captain signaled with his hand. First Lieutenant John Paul Jones hoisted a yellow silk flag bearing a picture of a rattlesnake and the motto, "Don't Tread on Me."

As the standard snapped in the crisp wind, the throngs crowding the waterfront responded with a boisterous cheer. Artillery ashore and afloat boomed out salutes. The Continental Navy was put into commission.

Eight vessels had hurriedly been converted from merchant ships. Their sides had been punctured for heavy guns, their holds refitted to accommodate larger crews.

BORN: April 26, 1718, Chopomisk, R.I.
DIED: February 26, 1802, Providence, R.I.

Commander in Chief Ezek Hopkins had his orders. He was to sail his fleet to Chesapeake Bay, Virginia, where three British warships, supported by a Tory navy of merchantmen, controlled the waters inside the Capes, endangering America's grip on Virginia and Maryland.

On January 4, 1776, flagships *Alfred*, *Cabot*, *Columbus*, and *Andrea Doria* left their moorings in Philadelphia. The little fleet cast a brave image as it sailed to nip the great naval power of Britain. But things can go wrong every which way with an untried fledgling. Very quickly the infant navy encountered difficulties.

Ice contested the passage down the Delaware River. After two weeks the ships had gone only as far as Reedy Island, where they came to a forlorn stop and lay icebound for a month. To prevent mass desertion, armed lieutenants stood watch day and night, gloomily stamping their feet and scissoring their arms in the bitter air. Sickness deepened the misery.

On the 14th, strengthened by sloop *Providence* and schooner *Fly*, the fleet arrived inside Cape Henlopen, where it welcomed the remaining two ships, sloop *Hornet* and schooner *Wasp*, altered in Baltimore. By then the mind of the Commander in Chief had steadied on a course of meek wisdom.

He had learned while still in Philadelphia that blustery weather had driven the British ships inside seaboard harbors. The coast was tricky and treacherous. Moreover, any engagement demanded that he act the aggressor, and under the sea-dog hide of Ezek Hopkins beat an unconquerable fondness for caution.

Luckily, his orders left a good deal to his discretion. He therefore signaled his ships and laid course for the Bahamas. He planned to capture guns and powder known to be in New Providence, whose defense rested now in the hands of civilians.

Once in trade waters, Hopkins felt more sure of himself, having served thirty-five years in the merchant service. He had fought during the French and Indian War and was as experienced an old salt as ever shook the topsail with profanity or clapped spyglass to the horizon—a Rhode Islander when the term meant "a born sailor." Notwithstanding this background, he owed his high appointment to his brother Stephen, a former governor and foremost citizen of Rhode Island.

At the outset of the Revolution the colonies boasted innumerable sea captains. All were schooled in the maritime, and none was trained for fleet command. Stephen, sitting on the Naval Committee, gained the top plum for Ezek, who three months before had been named brigadier general in charge of Rhode Island's yet-to-shoot military forces.

Had Congress intended Ezek Hopkins to be Commander in Chief of the Navy, equal to Washington on the seas, or simply to lead the eight-ship fleet? The extent of his authority is not clear. Nor is his title. Official documents refer to him sometimes as commodore (a courtesy title during the war), sometimes as admiral.

Regardless of the how or the what of his appointment, Ezek Hopkins made a fast, sure run south. By March 1, 1776, he had his goal in sight. He seized two sloops, secreted fifty sailors and two hundred marines aboard, and headed the captured vessels for Nassau harbor in a surprise attack.

The maneuver was a dandy, except that Hopkins had amateurishly displayed his fleet to the shore. Forewarned, Governor Montford Brown directed some civilians to fire a cannon, which scared off the two sloops. During the night the governor had one hundred and fifty casks of powder removed by a small sloop. The following day Hopkins landed and carried off a goodly supply of munitions, but only twenty-four barrels of precious powder.

The main objective of his mission had been blundered away.

With three officials as prisoners and his holds loaded with booty, Hopkins sailed for home. By April 3 he was off Long Island. Next day he captured two small vessels, and "had at sunset twelve sails." Success was mothering all flaws.

On the night of April 5–6, a new prize was sighted. The fleet encountered a single enemy, the twenty-gun H.M.S. *Glasgow*, bearing dispatches from Newport to Charleston. Hopkins' flaws, when scratched by a real fleet action, soon glared into the eye of posterity.

The old merchant sailor acted in an unswerving manner —flabbergasted. He formed no line of battle. His captains had to operate on their own. In the helter-skelter battle, *Glasgow* inflicted as much damage on the fleet as she suffered before making good her escape.

Hopkins arrived in New London on April 8 and was hailed as a hero by Congress and the press. But Washington met him and departed unimpressed, and his seamen were disgusted by the expedition. The doomed Captain Nicholas Biddle complained in a letter: "a more ill-conducted Affair never happened."

Hopkins laid ashore 202 sick. He obtained from Washington the brief loan of 170 soldiers in order to sail the fleet to Narragansett Bay, Rhode Island. A hundred more sailors sickened there, and the manpower shortage became crippling.

Hopkins managed to put two ships to sea (one under John Paul Jones) as raiders. The rest of the fleet swung idly in the bay for lack of hands. Two new ships were added, and gathered barnacles while Hopkins strove to recruit crews.

He appealed to the Rhode Island Assembly. Many of the legislators had interests in privateers, which needed sailors too. Hopkins was turned down, and the situation worsened. Men jumped the navy for the privateers, which paid higher wages and bigger and quicker shares of prize money.

Hopkins sweated, swore, and got nothing done. Amid a freshening blow of criticism, he kept asserting that if a better man could be found for the job, he would step aside for the good of the country. Congress, while declining to replace him, took a harder look at the Bahamas cruise and censured him.

The ultimate calamity fell in December. A British fleet sailed into Narragansett Bay. Several thousand Redcoats captured Newport and the surrounding territory. The hapless Continental fleet was blockaded.

The disgruntled officers of Hopkins' flagship *Warren* at last revolted. Captain John Grannis deserted the frigate and delivered the officers' complaints to Congress.

Hopkins was accused of calling Congress a pack of lawyers' clerks, among other charges. In turn, he blamed his stagnant warships on a conspiracy encouraged by the navy's great rivals, the privateer owners, whom he had caught diverting materials and laborers from naval construction to their own ships.

Congress denied Hopkins a hearing. Tired of the botchery, it suspended him on March 26, 1777, and formally dismissed him January 2, 1778.

The Bahamas cruise was virtually the only planned action undertaken by the Continental Navy. Not a year later the original fleet ended its short life in humiliation, ignobly bottled up in Narragansett Bay.

Altogether, fifty-three ships flew navy colors, performing usually as independent commerce raiders. Privateers waged the most punishing war on the waters. About two thousand of these privately owned vessels, manned by seventy thousand sailors, caused British merchant marine losses of $18,000,000. The money filled the pockets of the owners, not the echoing hollow of the Treasury, however.

Additionally, eleven states had navies, of which the majority were jealously employed in guarding their own coasts and waterways.

Like Ward, Schuyler, and Putnam, Ezek Hopkins was devoted but inadequate. Launching a navy required another Washington. Hopkins stepped in up to his neck and foundered.

He finished his life on land, respected by his fellows. Over his grave was erected a heroic bronze statue. It represents him in the uniform of the first and last Commander in Chief of the Continental Navy.

JOHANN SEUME
Detour to Paris

JOHANN SEUME WAS FINDING LIFE MORE UNBEARABLE
each day.

A theological student at Leipzig, he had the heart of
a poet. He valued his friends, and being a sensitive youth,
he did not wish to offend them by voicing his religious
doubts.

So one morning Seume packed several shirts and a few
classics into a knapsack, dropped nine talers into his
pocket, and with sword at his belt started on foot for Paris
and a new life.

His trip was to be longer than he anticipated.

The third night he stopped at Bach. Two stalwart
soldiers approached him. They were recruiting officers for
that seller of souls, the Landgrave of Hesse-Cassel, who
was corralling men for the British army. The officers
disarmed Seume and put him under arrest. They tore up
his academic papers, his only proof of identity, and hustled
him off to a prisonlike garrison in Ziegenhayn.

BORN: Date and place uncertain
DIED: Date and place uncertain

Seume had ample company in misery. His unfortunate companies included political undesirables, drunkards, troublemakers, vagabonds, cashiered officers, bankrupt merchants, and a good number of harmless but luckless fellows like himself. No one, concluded Seume, was safe from the Landgrave.

With Germanic stolidness and just a dash of poetic philosophy, he reflected that "the idea of crossing the ocean was inviting enough to a young fellow, and there were things worth seeing on the other side."

Reconciled to his fate, Johann Seume found himself in good time aboard a British ship standing out for the New World.

The voyage was not represented as a pleasure cruise. Six men were assigned to a berth intended to accommodate four. Meals consisted mainly of rotting pork or salt beef and foul peas. Ships biscuits housed whole families of maggots and often were so hard that use of a cannonball was necessary to chip them. Water had to be strained through a handkerchief before it was drinkable.

The English Quartermaster Department assigned no corner of its jurisdiction to comfort, and the greed of the German rulers did not suffer from the enervations of conscience. The Duke of Brunswick had already shipped two thousand soldiers to Quebec without overcoats and with shoes that did not stick together. Nineteen Brunswickers died and 131 fell sick of scurvy before the wretches reached Canada.

Johann Seume was one of nearly thirty thousand Germans purchased to fight against Americans. England's peacetime army lacked the size to quell an overseas rebellion, and recruiting lagged woefully. An attempt was first made to hire twenty thousand Russians. Empress Catherine refused. The Dutch and Frederick the Great of Prussia would have none of a buildup in English might, either. Lord North, the prime minister, then turned to

Germany, long the stock farm of European soldiery.

Germany at this time was a patchwork of three hundred petty kingdoms. Britain signed mail-order contracts with six of the largest: Brunswick, Hesse-Cassel, Hesse-Hanau, Waldeck, Anspach-Bayreuth, and Anhalt-Zerbst.

Deals varied with each state. According to the first contract, with the Duke of Brunswick, England paid more than eleven thousand pounds to start, and double that sum for two years. The Duke also received "head money" of more than seven pounds for each man furnished. A similar sum was paid for each man killed, and three wounded counted as one killed. All told, the Duke sent 5,723 men to America. He urged them to brave the thick of battle where casualties in wounded and dead swelled his purse. Deserters fetched no blood money. Desertion, consequently, became the blackest of crimes in the Duke's journal.

The Landgrave of Hesse-Cassel dredged up 16,992 men, more than the other five states together. He received twice as much per man as the Duke of Brunswick but apparently no blood money. Hessians proved to be the ablest fighters. Because of their ferocity and numbers, the word "Hessian" came to stand for all the Germans who fought in the Revolution.

The sale of mercenaries loaded the treasuries of the six German courts and kept their rulers in Wienerschnitzels, sauerkraut, Rhenish wine, and women. These princelings cared nothing for the manner in which their regiments were filled, though the use of force—at least within the home state—was mildly opposed.

Recruiting officers constantly lost their way, crossed borders, and found their way back, with honest farm boys in tow. Men eligible for duty in America were not difficult to spot from afar. A recruit had to be less than sixty years of age and strong enough to walk.

To simplify their tasks, recruiting officers had the assistance of savage dogs and a manual. In the latter were

described the precautions necessary to bring a recruit
safely into garrison.

The recruit must walk in front (the manual stipulated),
never in the rear, and he must be aware that one false step
might cost him his life. The officer must dodge places
where the recruit is known. Nights must be spent only at
inns whose landlords are friendly. The recruit must enter
a building or door first and leave last. During the night
both officer and prisoner must give up their clothes to the
landlord. The officer must yield his weapons, too, lest the
recruit steal them while he sleeps. Should a recruit cause
trouble, the buttons and straps must be snipped from his
pants, compelling him to use both hands to preserve his
decency. Finally, should an officer be obliged to slay a
troublemaker, he must obtain a paper from the local
magistrate. No paper, however, excused the *escape* of a
recruit.

The best German regiments arrived in America early,
in 1776. As the war progressed, the despots had to scratch
and scrape. The Landgrave of Hesse-Cassel, greediest of
the greedy, in desperation stripped his own land of a fourth
of its manpower. One of his generals, Wilhelm von Kyn-
phausen, complained that among the new regiments
pilfering from one other and plundering of Americans
raged nearly out of control.

Only after bitter debate did Parliament pass the motion
to employ German mercenaries. Members of the opposition
party, the Whigs, had pointed out that the use of Germans
would convince the Americans to discard their allegiance
to the British throne and to seek an alliance with their old
enemies, the French.

The danger that the lords feared became a reality. The
rebel army received decisive help from France. And one
of the grievances that Thomas Jefferson wrote into the
Declaration of Independence was that the King "is at this

time, transporting large armies of foreign mercenaries to complete the works of death, desolation, and tyranny."

George Washington actively supported a psychological warfare aimed at persuading the Germans to desert. He made certain that German prisoners were treated extremely well so that when exchanged, they might spread the propaganda. He offered lands as inducement to quit the British army and settle in America. These offers ranged from one thousand acres for colonels to fifty acres for privates.

The British countered. The Americans, they insisted, gave no quarter in battle; any German lucky enough to be taken prisoner would be sold into slavery. Accusations flew, and the worst were believed on both sides. When Hessians landed in Newport, the townspeople bolted their doors in panic, having been told that Hessians ate little children.

The German, despite his enforced recruiting, made a dependable soldier. Trained to doglike obedience, he looked with a harsh eye on people who rebelled. He fought in the major battles and he usually fought well, being wisely kept to his own regiments. Still, about five thousand remained in America.

Johann Seume, the disillusioned theological student, returned home with seventeen thousand other Germans and became a well-known writer. He is typical of the German mercenary only in the manner of his impressment. Stephan Popp, who went home to become a traveling musician and the father of nine children, is a truer example of the German who lost seven years of his life fighting somebody else's war.

Popp came from Anspach, where no subject could marry or leave the country without permission. He marched out of Yorktown a prisoner. During the next six months in captivity he had "often more lice than clothing." Docilely he endured and docilely he remembered.

When imprisoned at Frederick, Maryland, he noted in his diary for April 30, 1782:

"We celebrated at the customary times the birthdays of our prince and his wife as best we could. We made an illumination all over, burning more than 200 to 300 lights."

JOHN HANCOCK
Patriot with a Purse

AFTER THREE DAYS OF ARGUING, THE RESOLUTION HAD passed.

In the ground floor chamber of the red brick State House in Philadelphia, Charles Thomson, secretary of the Second Continental Congress, recorded the vote and handed the paper to rich and fussy John Hancock III. Hancock signed it as President. Thomson added his name.

None of the delegates stood on chairs and shouted. In a businesslike tone Hancock ordered the Declaration of Independence, with its two signatures, printed and framed. He directed that copies be sent to all important persons and assemblies. Then he rapped his gavel smartly. Time was winging, and there was other work to be done.

By late that afternoon of July 4, 1776, the calendar was completed. The last item, the sale of twenty-five pounds of powder to a North Carolina man, was approved. The air had cooled. The whir of horseflies had subsided. Hancock adjourned the meeting.

BORN: January 16 (?), 1737, Braintree, Mass.
DIED: October 8, 1793, Boston, Mass.

He pushed himself erect—a man slender and handsome and garbed, like the merchant prince he was, in rainbow stockings and embroidered satin waistcoat. Slowly, on painful joints, he walked outside. Although not quite forty, he stooped under the many ailments that were prematurely aging him.

One of his splendid coaches awaited him on the street. Somewhere beyond it a hangman's noose might also be waiting. King George III would overlook Thomson's signature; it merely attested to the President's. Hancock, idol of the people and arch traitor, was something else. He was the ideal man to make an example of.

John Hancock was accustomed to risking his life. Had he and Sam Adams been captured during the days pointing toward Lexington and Concord, their heads might have adorned London Bridge. Only he and Adams had been excluded from the general pardon offered by General Gage to woo the rebels back into the King's fold.

Adams, that fanatic of revolution, had fished carefully for Hancock. The early patriotic movement had desperately needed a figurehead and a financier. Hancock was both, and more. He had ungloved the hand of a master politician. Foes called him "a shallow head and a deep purse." Yet they could not fault the plush-smooth way he ran Congress.

As he moved upon gouty legs from the State House to his coach, people stopped and gaped. In Philadelphia, as in his native Boston, the populace regarded him with awe and pride.

A liveried coachman cracked his whip. The perfectly matched bays pranced forward. Off sped "King Hancock" with a wave of his soft hand. He doted on the admiration and gratitude of the people. A thousand families depended on the House of Hancock for their daily bread and shelter.

He was a democrat who lived like an aristocrat, and the masses adored him for it. Unlike many wealthy colonials, he had not opposed change, he had not sided with the King. To have the richest man in New England throw in with them gave the rabble a sheath of luster for their cause.

Just why did John Hancock make America's business his business? Did he expect that a short-term sacrifice now would return him tenfold when the colonies set up business for themselves?

Or was there another reason? Did he admit that reason only to himself—that he was a mediocre businessman?

The House of Hancock was not of his building. Everything was inherited from an uncle, Thomas Hancock, loyalist and occasional smuggler. John had turned the war-wounded enterprises over to a manager. He had placed himself on the one open road to authority and renown—politics. Boosted by wealth and high position, he had climbed rapidly. On the way, he had advanced the arts, manufacturing, and agriculture.

As President of Congress he showed gifts both of tongue and pen. And as the heat blazed off the streets of Philadelphia in the summer of 1776, he was nearing that flourish of pen which would fix his fame.

July went out. On August 2, the formal parchment copy of the Declaration of Independence lay ready for signatures. For the second time Hancock signed it, the first of fifty-six Americans.

His beautiful, copper-plate signature, underlined with a flourish, appears at the top. It is nearly twice as large as any other, and half again as large as he normally wrote.

"There!" he exclaimed, resting his pen. "John Bull can read my name without spectacles and may now double his reward of five hundred pounds on my head!"

Two months later Hancock stepped down from the Presidency for reasons of health. His term of two years and five months was marked by a suave ability to knit together dangerous factions. And by his "political gout."

This special version of gout was famous for its sensitivity to debates on key issues. During attacks, he retired to his chambers to lie down. When the popular trend became clear, he emerged and committed himself.

The ex-President's vanity bore up manfully despite his failing legs. He had to travel through Tory-ridden towns in order to reach his home in Boston. Blithely he wrote Washington for an escort of light horse. Washington had his mind on the setbacks at Brandywine and Germantown, and army horses were scarce. Nonetheless, he sent twelve dragoons and an apology for the guard "being so small."

Once home, Hancock refurbished his mansion, which had been damaged during a British occupation. The house, the first on Beacon Hill, was fashioned of granite and cornered with freestone. Here in the days before Concord angry British soldiers had hacked at the fences, threatened bodily harm, and bragged that everything would soon be theirs. Hancock added a wing with a banquet hall, where in later years he was to entertain as governor.

His political enemies hoped that King Hancock had retired for good to his magnificent stone castle, to his jug of hot rum punch (a fixture night and day on his sideboard), to his beloved Madeira wine, and his lavish meals.

Such hopes were empty. The strangely aging fashion plate doffed his lavender coat for a red velvet cap and red Morocco slippers. But he retained his patriotic vigor.

He remained a member of Congress, spent more and more time in Boston, and suddenly blossomed as a soldier. He had always fancied himself a military talent. The nomination of Washington to lead the army had shocked him, for he had envisioned the position as his. Making the grand flourish, he had offered himself to Washington in any capacity, "be it to take the firelock and join the ranks as a volunteer."

As he had foreseen, the offer was graciously turned down.

In a more honest moment he had written to a confederate to "send my commission as major-general that I may appear in character."

In August, 1780, General Hancock took the field with a personal suite and five thousand Massachusetts volunteers. Unfortunately he chose the wrong campaign, the Rhode Island expedition. While his men deserted, Hancock entertained his friends, and except for wet feet and headaches, thoroughly enjoyed the life of the gentleman soldier. The expedition collapsed in sorry failure, though for reasons apart from Hancock's generalship.

After this one outing, Hancock returned to the political arena. He was overwhelmingly elected first governor of Massachusetts, a position at the time of highest prestige. He was reelected annually (except in two years) until his death in 1794.

As governor he stayed in close touch with all classes, juggling work and pleasure. His laws relieving the plight of debtors became a model for the rest of the country. Dignitaries involved in the Franco-American wartime alliance eased their tensions at his extravagant fetes on Beacon Hill.

Perhaps his greatest contribution to America came after the Revolution. In 1788 he was instrumental in persuading Massachusetts, a critical state, to ratify the Federal Constitution, though he himself was an ardent states' rights man.

John Adams, alternately friend and enemy, lifted Hancock's name beside those of James Otis and Sam Adams as the "firmest pillars of the whole revolution." Certainly Hancock deserves a place beside the select few who served their country before, during, and after the war.

He died in his fifty-fourth year. Thousands viewed his body as it lay in state at Beacon Hill. On the day of his funeral, every store in Boston closed in his honor. Every militiaman turned out. Twenty thousand mourners marched in the mile and a half procession to the grave in Old Granary Burying Ground.

It was fitting. Flamboyant John Hancock departed as he had done everything.

With a flourish.

CHARLES LEE
Rebel from England

ENGLISH-BORN CHARLES LEE FELT NO UNEASINESS ABOUT
his choice of headquarters for the night, nor about the date.

The tavern kept by the widow Mrs. White in Basking
Bridge, New Jersey, was neat and warm. His troops camped
three miles away, a distance safe enough with the enemy
under Cornwallis some twenty miles off.

The day, Friday the 13th, bothered Lee not one goose
pimple. Superstition had no part in his rise to the position
of number two general in the Continental Army. His
experience in the British service and a pompous sense of
his own ability had awed Congress. Zealous patriots put
as much faith in him as in Washington. And some—with
Lee's approval—more.

Around eight o'clock a troop of Connecticut mounted
militia rode by the tavern. Lee wasted precious time ranting
at them for wearing wigs. Finally he scribbled orders for
the day.

BORN: January (?), 1732 (?), Chester, England
DIED: October 2, 1782, Philadelphia, Pa.

Leisurely he returned to his room, knowing that Washington, retreating from Howe across New Jersey, clamored for his assistance. Lee was in no rush to aid his chief. For days he had delayed joining Washington in the hope of winning individual laurels by harassing Cornwallis.

Nibbling at a breakfast plate, Lee wrote a bitter letter to his fellow malcontent, General Horatio Gates. The war, stated Lee, was grossly mismanaged for want of heeding his advice. Washington was described in the letter as "a certain great man" who "is most damnably deficient."

Lee had scarcely signed his name when over by an end window Captain James Wilkinson gave a cry.

On the lane that led from the main road to the tavern was the startling spectacle of British dragoons.

"Here, sir, are the British cavalry!"

"Where?" gasped Lee.

"Around the house," answered Wilkinson, seeing the British circling.

Lee cursed. "Where is the guard? Why don't they fire?"

Wilkinson hastened to find out. A hail of bullets greeted him at the front door. He ducked back.

The surprised guards were separated from their arms, which they had carelessly left in a room of the tavern. Banastre Tarleton, second-in-command of the raiders, shouted to his twenty-eight Redcoats to "cut up as many as they could."

For several minutes Lee paced an upper chamber while his aides returned shot for shot.

"If the general does not surrender in five minutes, I will set fire to the house," called Tarleton, who was beginning to make a career of ferocity.

Mrs. White pleaded that her property be spared. Tarleton merely repeated the warning.

After a short pause, one of Lee's aides bawled: "Here is the general. He has surrendered."

General Charles Lee appeared. Humiliation pinched his dark, bony face, making his great beak of a nose seem larger than ever. Always the sloven, he wore a blanket coat and slippers. His collar lay open, and his shirt was soiled with several days' wear.

Quickly the British mounted him on Captain Wilkinson's horse. (Wilkinson hid in a chimney with the letter to Gates and escaped detection.) A bugle sounded, ending the fifteen-minute skirmish. The raiders conducted their prize to Lord Cornwallis at Penning.

The reaction to Lee's kidnapping was widespread and varied. His jubilant captors celebrated by getting his horse drunk. Washington gravely asserted that "our cause . . . received a severe blow." In England, many believed the end of the war had come.

Deprived of Lee, the professional soldier, the cause of liberty dimmed nearly to darkness. Early in the war John Adams, a miser with praise, had written the general: "We want you at New York—we want you at Cambridge— we want you in Virginia." But thirteen days after the calamity at Mrs. White's tavern, George Washington crossed the Delaware and smashed the Germans at Trenton. Suddenly it dawned on many that Lee was not the indispensable man.

Still, he was not without skill and courage. His performances during the first eighteen months of war (at Boston, Rhode Island, New York, Virginia, and Charleston) were creditable. He believed them glorious—and himself the logical Commander in Chief. As a former lieutenant colonel in the British army, he looked down his huge nose at the country amateurs who officered the Americans.

This disdain, plus the deep-rooted hold of his English birth and military training, hampered his usefulness in combat. He feared that the patriots must fall before the

British regulars in a pitched battle. Consequently he thought along defensive lines, of wearing the enemy down by guerilla-type tactics.

As a prisoner he received handsome treatment. Yet he pined for the company of his dogs. Around the rebel camps he had cut a unique sight, a skinny figure dressed in a battered cocked hat, split shirt, and greasy breeches, trailed everywhere by a pack of dogs. He wrote Washington requesting his canine companies, and one mongrel was sent him.

With a friend by his side, he talked at length with the top British officers. The Declaration of Independence, he asserted, was not meant to be a permanent statement of purpose. The colonies really did not want independence, but freedom within the British Empire.

He wrote as well as talked, for he wielded a clever pen. In happier days he had composed love notes, charming and winsome. Alas, these could not counter his homeliness, and his suit was invariably rejected. As a pamphleteer, he had assailed the government of King George, first in England and then in America, where he came to live in 1773. Now, as a prisoner of the British, he wrote in a very different mood.

On March 29, 1777, he completed his most famous literary endeavor. It was a plan detailing how the British could defeat the Americans. The plan was ignored. But Lee had a hard time explaining it away to the Americans afterward. It was, he insisted, a hoax intended to mislead his British captors into wasting their strength in futile campaigns.

The mind of Charles Lee may have actually come to believe his own alibi. Decidedly, he was a most confused Englishman. The shame of his captivity had aggravated old afflictions: the pain of rheumatism and gout, the stab of unrequited love, the disappointment over the lack of promotion in the British army, the loneliness of a worldly intellectual among provincials. Had he really been fighting for freedom in general—or *freedom for himself?*

In April, 1778, Lee was exchanged after sixteen months as a prisoner. He joined Washington's army at Valley Forge in May on the eve of the Monmouth campaign.

Washington had determined to take the offensive against the British. He proffered the honor of leading the attack to Lee, the senior major general. Lee declined, still believing the Americans had no chance in a stand-up battle with British regulars. At the last minute Lee reconsidered rather than let slip away the opportunity of redeeming his reputation.

Monmouth tested Lee's mastery over a large-scale battle. It found the man in the dirty uniform wanting. He simply lost control of the action. The Americans had begun to run when Washington arrived. Aghast at the situation, the Commander in Chief "swore till the leaves shook on the trees." He ordered Lee to the rear, re-formed his men, and held the British till night ended the fighting.

A court-martial suspended Lee for twelve months. His reputation in tatters, he hung around Philadelphia, railing at Congress and Washington. So insulting did he wax that he was dismissed from the army on January 10, 1780.

Disgraced, he struggled through two years benighted by ill health and disillusionment. He turned his pen to creating an ideal republic of farmers and soldiers in which he figured importantly. He volleyed abuses with a horde of foes, once so losing control of himself that he chased a publisher down Market Street with a horsewhip.

"Great God," he wrote to his sister, "what a dupe and victim I have been to the . . . name of liberty!"

Charles Lee, widely considered the most competent commander in the Continental Army during the first year and a half of war, died in a cheap tavern.

Two faithful dogs vainly tried to wake him.

JOHN GLOVER

Johnny-on-the-Spot

TOWARD SUNSET THE RIVER BEGAN TO CROWD UP. SMALL boats for miles around—fishing craft collected from the Long Island Sound, barges, skiffs, and scows brought down from the North River—all were funneling into the East River. Anything and everything that floated was going to the rescue of the Continental Army.

Washington had issued the orders. To General Heath and Hugh Hughes, assistant Quartermaster General, had gone the job of assembling all the boats they could lay their hands on. To Colonel John Glover had gone the edict: save the army.

On August 27, 1776, two days earlier, the Americans had been routed in the first battle for New York. They had been chased, sobbing and exhausted, into their breastworks at Brooklyn Heights. Only the memory of costly Bunker Hill had kept the British generals from hurling the frontal assault for which the German mercenaries had begged.

BORN: November 5, 1732, Salem, Mass.
DIED: January 30, 1797, Marblehead, Mass.

Instead, Britain's General Howe had adopted siege tactics. On the 29th he had begun digging his first parallel scarcely one hundred and fifty rods from colonial lines. In a matter of time the rebels, clinging for life to a mile-square patch of open ground, would be shoved off Long Island and into the sea.

Washington recovered slowly from the shock of his first defeat. He rode along the riverbank observing the cream of his reinforcements—Colonel John Glover and the 14th Continental Regiment. Everything now depended on how they manned the boats.

The 14th was an infantry regiment muscled by rugged fishermen and sailors, chiefly from Marblehead, Massachusetts. Accustomed to life at sea and its constant dangers, they made the ideal men for the emergency. The feel of oar and tiller was good after months of landlubber duty.

At the helm of the 14th stood redheaded John Glover. A scrappy little merchant mariner, he ran his unit with a sea captain's iron hand. By ten that night he had the desperate ferry service under way.

It was to be a race against time and threatening elements. The complex retreat had to be accomplished before the British awoke to the stratagem. In one night —and midsummer nights are short—Glover's seafarers, aided by those of Israel Hutchinson, had to snatch from the precarious beachhead upward of ten thousand troops.

In pitch-blackness, across a mile of unfamiliar water and back again, the skilled Marblehead men maneuvered boatload after boatload. Every prow that nosed unerringly into shore paid tribute to Glover, and to Washington.

One by one each regiment was pulled from the line and told a secret: it alone was being relieved. Each regiment stole in tomblike silence to the waterfront, fearing not so much the enemy as their unlucky comrades who, hearing

their footsteps, might ruin all chance for their survival by a
mass stampede.

Washington's beautifully simple scheme worked for a
time. A northeasterly wind prevented the British fleet
from sailing unopposed up the East River. Then shortly
before midnight, the wind shifted. Glover's sailing vessels
were useless, and there were too few rowboats. Agonizing
minutes drifted away unused. Just as the whole enterprise
seemed overtaken by disaster, the favorable wind returned.

Glover kept his seagoing soldiers at their labor while he
anxiously scanned the horizon for signs of dawn. The force
on the Brooklyn side grew smaller and smaller.

With the daylight a friendly fog unfurled, hiding the
evacuation of the rear guard. When the air cleared, General
Howe and his officers, caught flatfooted, viewed the
abandoned works with amazement and chagrin.

The men who had been penned on the Brooklyn beachhead represented the pick of the Continental Army. Joined
to the seven thousand troops on Manhattan (four thousand
were spread through New Jersey), the army was again
intact and ready to fight another day. Glover and his
fishermen had saved what the Lexington and Concord
farmers had started. And on the stormy night of August
29-30, 1776, the United States amphibious corps was born.

Catching the enemy unaware became a specialty of
John Glover's. Not only did he execute Washington's most
frantic defensive stroke, the Long Island retreat, but he
played the key role in Washington's boldest offensive
thrust—the attack at Trenton. He and his men ferried the
army across the Delaware despite enforced silence, total
blackout, and a new hazard—chunks of ice as deadly as
torpedoes.

"The floating ice in the river made the labor almost
incredible," marveled Henry Knox. Years later the artillery
chief recalled the crossing and the subsequent performance
of the Marbleheaders in the vanguard of the Trenton attack.

"I wish the members of this body," he said in a speech before the Massachusetts legislature, "had stood on the banks of the Delaware . . . in that bitter night . . . and seen the men from Marblehead, and Marblehead alone, stand forward to lead the army along the perilous path to . . . Trenton. There, sir, went the fishermen of Marblehead, alike at home upon land or water . . . ardent, patriotic, and unflinching."

That he could command alike upon land or water John Glover had demonstrated brilliantly.

Some two weeks after the hairbreadth Long Island retreat, the British landed at Kip's Bay in the center of Manhattan. The patriots fled in sheer terror—all except Glover's regiment, which had hurried down from Harlem. Their stand halted the British long enough to stave off a debacle. Washington's faith in the American fighting man was restored.

The following month Glover saved the American army from encirclement at Pelham Bay. His brigade of seven hundred and fifty men and three field pieces was isolated from the main body. Acting on his own, he gave fight to a landing party of some four thousand. Although out-numbered nearly five to one, he kept his one-hundred-eighty-man regiment in reserve. He fought the rest so fiercely that his opponent, Henry Clinton, swore he faced fourteen thousand troops.

Again at Quaker Hill (siege of Newport) in August, 1777, he delayed the onrushing British. His unit alone stood firm and probably allowed the ill-starred Rhode Island expedition to withdraw to the mainland and escape annihilation.

Who was John Glover? Who was this Johnny-on-the-spot, this panic-proof human anchor during the chaos of retreat?

Born in Salem, Massachusetts, in 1732 (the same year as Washington), Glover was removed by his parents to

Marblehead when still a tot. In his early twenties he worked as a cordwainer. Like all ambitious colonial artisans, he became a jack-of-all-trades.

Prospering in fisheries and as a shipowner, he established himself as a leading member of the "codfish aristocracy," the ruling class of Marblehead. He joined the right clubs, built his mansion, fathered eleven children, and became one of the triumvirate that dominated local politics.

Self-confident, self-made, and dashing (he fancied twin silver pistols and a Scottish broadsword), Glover commanded in the field with the power of mind that had won him financial success. His troops behaved with discipline rare in the early part of the war. Continental officers who ordinarily had little respect for "Yankees" had respect for the 14th.

The Marbleheaders played as stoutly as they warred. Roughhouse amusements invariably accompanied their white caps, blue jackets, and tarred trousers. When Dan Morgan's colorfully dressed riflemen arrived in the camps at Cambridge, a nose-to-nose rivalry ensued. After a few passes at fisticuffs the swaggering frontiersmen contented themselves with long-distance snarling.

If the briny deep gave Glover and his men hardiness, it also gave them independence. After Trenton, the 14th Regiment disbanded. Like most sailors of the Revolution, the Marbleheaders went back to sea. On a privateer's deck a man could slip a small fortune under the cloak of patriotism.

Glover himself was a reluctant patriot after Trenton. And after the Rhode Island campaign he did not engage in heavy fighting. He did garrison service in Providence, field duty in the Hudson Highlands, and mustered recruits in Massachusetts.

For the last five years he tried to quit the service and was finally retired before the close of hostilities. He pleaded shattered health ("I could not ride a horse five miles") and poverty (he was owed two years' pay).

As a civilian he regained both health and fortune in giant strides. He died at sixty-five, leaving his heirs well provided. He left, too, the first chapter of American amphibious warfare, written on the dark and silent waters of the East River and the Delaware.

PHILIP SCHUYLER

To the Manor Born

THE PACKET *General Wall*, HER CAPTAIN DYING, WANDERED aimlessly in mid-Atlantic in the winter of 1761.

Her crew consisted of the sweepings of tavern floors and back alleys, and none of them knew how to navigate, a state of vacancy that was edging the passengers toward hysterics.

Someone remembered Philip Schuyler, a rather aloof passenger who had plunked himself by the sternpost when the ship departed New York. Since then he had scarcely lifted his nose from a book on navigation borrowed from the captain. Schuyler was called from the captain's side and asked to assume command.

He had never skippered anything longer than a flatboat on the Hudson River. A taste for mathematics and a distaste for his commonplace shipmates had prompted his withdrawal into nautical studies. He had learned well. He guided the packet within sight of the European coast,

Born: November 11, 1733, Albany, N.Y.
Died: November 18, 1804, Albany, N.Y.

where adventures piled up. The *General Wall* was captured
by a French privateer and retaken by a British frigate in
petty actions of the Seven Years' War. Schuyler and his
fellow passengers eventually reached London safely.

During the Revolution twenty years later Philip Schuyler
was again thrust into an emergency in which he alone
could save those about him. This time it was not a shipload
of lowborn strangers whom death threatened, but his own
family in his own mansion.

His patriotism had so maddened the Tories and their
Indian allies that one night they broke into his home.
Margaret Schuyler, running with her little sister in her
arms, ducked a flying tomahawk that stuck in the staircase
railing.

Schuyler herded his family into an upper room and
poured out a hot volley of musketry. As ammunition ran
low, he called out orders from a window, pretending to
direct a rescue party. The raiders had already had enough
of the determined old man. Stealing the family silver, they
fled into the night.

In navigating the *General Wall* halfway across the ocean
Philip Schuyler had demonstrated confidence, intelligence,
and willingness to shoulder responsibility. In defending
his home, he had displayed courage and quickness of mind.
Between the two episodes in 1761 and 1781 erupted the
Revolution with its crying need for men of his talents.

Add to his talents a varied experience in the French and
Indian War and a distinguished background as heir to one
of America's great landholding families. Add that he
started at the top: as Washington's friend, as the third of
the four original major generals authorized by Congress.

The sum ought to have lifted him into the forefront of
Revolutionary heroes. Yet he resigned from the army in
1779, four years before the peace treaty, his patriotism,
sacrifices, and talents dissipated in endless squabbles.

Physically this man who should have been an immortal was slender of body and large of feature. He moved with an energy that belied his rheumatic gout, an ailment suffered since boyhood. Poor health may partly explain his irritability and impatience; unquestionably it robbed him of his great chance.

He could be a model of patience and courtesy with men of his social standing. He entertained as a houseguest John Burgoyne after the British general's surrender, albeit Burgoyne had needlessly burned one of his stately mansions to the ground. To men of inferior class who bucked him, Schuyler reacted with contempt. He thus created friction everywhere. The Continental Army boasted few other men who owned almost limitless real estate, renting yearly at two hundred pounds per hundred acres.

"The general is somewhat haughty and overbearing," the Rev. Cotton Mather Smith wrote to his wife in July, 1775. "He has never been accustomed to seeing men that are reasonably well taught, and able to give a clear opinion, and to state their grounds for it, who were not also persons of some wealth and rank."

When a blacksmith approached him at Ticonderoga to offer some information, Schuyler dismissed him without a hearing. Smith, who was standing close by, wrote that "it was not until I had explained to him that the man was well descended and only a blacksmith by reason that his grandfather's English estates had been forfeited to the crown that the General could be prevailed upon to listen to him."

When early in the war Allen and Arnold captured Fort Ticonderoga, Congress saw the door to Canada standing ajar. England could be taught that she faced more than a defensive war. Schuyler received the commission of organizing and leading an invasion.

Congress naïvely handicapped him by decreeing that

New York should provide most of the supplies and Connecticut most of the men. The Connecticut troops smarted at being under a New Yorker, especially a "stupid Dutchman" with fancy airs. Rivalry between New Englanders and Yorkers had long smoldered over the contested New Hampshire Grants. In the closeness of the army, everything aggravated the old hatreds—from the choice of campsites to Connecticut flour going to New York troops.

The bickering and insubordination exasperated Schuyler, who had learned to appreciate the fruits of discipline without caring to get down to earth to plant the seeds.

His health broke. He turned over the immediate command of the invasion force to Richard Montgomery and bade farewell to his greatest opportunity.

Montgomery took Montreal on November 13, 1775, and died in the snow before Quebec. The invaders tramped back to Crown Point, cursing and name-calling.

Yankees in western Massachusetts and Connecticut held protest meetings and singled out Schuyler, the rich Yorker. He was accused of being a Tory and of neglecting the men in Canada in order to ensure their defeat. The money intended for their care he was said to have slipped into his own pocket.

While slurs discolored the air, a new adversary slid up from Philadelphia. A crafty opportunist, Horatio Gates, had inveigled the Congress into naming him Montgomery's successor. Before he could take the field, however, the troops were back under Schuyler's jurisdiction. Never one to shrink from another man's porridge, Gates intrigued for Schuyler's entire Northern Department.

Proud, lofty Philip Schuyler was now engaged on three fronts. He had his military operations to prepare. He had to defend himself from the slander of those New England fishmongers. And he had to parry the whittling of the tirelessly ambitious Horatio Gates.

The land baron won no place. He vanquished Gates temporarily, though it needed months of threatened resignations, appeals for a court of inquiry, and finally a cloudy vindication of his conduct by Congress.

Seated as sole commander of the Northern Department, he strung together a makeshift army. Without a single cannon, he moved to contest Burgoyne's invasion from Canada.

Schuyler planned shrewdly to fight in retreat and to harass the British column till new levies of militia tipped the balance of manpower his way. One moment of hesitation at the beginning marred the excellent scheme and cost Fort Ticonderoga.

New Englanders cranked their rumor machines day and night: Schuyler and his chief aide, Arthur St. Clair, had sold out the fort—Burgoyne had shot silver balls into the American camp, and St. Clair had chased after them and divided the loot with Schuyler.

Unnerved by the loss of Fort Ticonderoga and dinned by the fantastic charges, Congress removed Schuyler. Gates took over. Performing on Schuyler's plans, he compelled Burgoyne to surrender at Saratoga.

Schuyler pressed demands for a formal hearing to restore his good name. In October, 1778, he was completely cleared by a court-martial. The following April he resigned from the army, but remained active in the cause of independence.

His forcefulness as a member of the Board of Commissioners for Indian Affairs incited the savage attack on his home and family. He helped reorganize the staff departments of the army. He worked to improve relations with the French troops.

In peace he represented New York in the first United States Senate, where he championed the financial program of his son-in-law, Alexander Hamilton. In 1798, after a vigorous public life, he retired to his various domains in

Saratoga, along the Mohawk, in Dutchess County, and at Cortland Manor.

There once again he was the great lord whose patriotism and sacrifice could not be twisted by fishmongers.

Once more his homes provided sumptuous receptions for aristocrats from all parts of the Western world.

Except New England.

MARQUIS DE LAFAYETTE

Enchanter from France

A BAND OF THIRTEEN ADVENTURERS STOOD ON THE HIGH
poop of *La Victoire* and watched the hilly skyline of Spain
recede behind them. The little frigate was bearing some of
the Frenchmen to death, some to a dusty niche of military
fame, and one to a career of purest romance.

La Victoire crossed the sleepy waters of Pasajes Bay and
pitched alarmingly in the rough sea of the Bay of Biscayne.
Thrown against the taffrail, young Marie Joseph Paul
Yves Roch Gilbert du Motier, Marquis de Lafayette, felt
an inner pang to go with the hard jolt of the railing.

Had he acted too rashly in embarking upon this shaky
little tub for a voyage of two months? Of the American
people and their cause he knew, really, almost nothing.
But of Paris . . . ah! Was his name already on every tongue
in Paris?

A few short hours ago he had been galloping on European
soil. And only two years earlier he had been a captain

BORN: September 6, 1757, Château of Chavaniac, France
DIED: May 20, 1834, Paris, France

serving with his regiment in the no-place German town of
Metz. There he had first heard of the brave revolt of the
thirteen colonies. France was neutral, and so Lafayette,
aflame with the spirit of knight-errantry, could not sail to
the rescue as a French officer. Putting forth his wealth, he
had purchased a ship and collected a staff. When the
French King tried to stop him, he had moved *La Victoire*
to a Spanish port.

He had barely escaped imprisonment by donning the
jackboots and livery of a courier and galloping to reach
his ship.

It had been a risky extravaganza all the way. Would it
turn out well? Behind were his native land, his irate King,
his seventeen-year-old wife of three years. With him he
carried the promise of a commission as major general in
the Continental Army bestowed by American agent Silas
Deane. Beyond the Atlantic lay a chance to pay back
England for the humiliating defeat of the Seven Years'
War, a chance to add to the glory of France, and perchance
to the glory of Lafayette. Surely the King would forgive
him for acting on his own—aye, kiss him!

The clumsy little craft pitched dreadfully. Seasick, the
young nobleman wondered if his impulsive act might *not*
be forgiven at court. Again the ship fell away beneath his
legs. Gilbert Lafayette, nineteen, forlornly went below and
slammed the hatch.

Days passed amid the blankness of sea and sky. Monotony
always made him melancholy. He brooded upon the tales
of poverty in every corner of his homeland—French peasants who cut their fruit trees for firewood and baked dry
the green wheat in order to eat. The oppressed in life
stirred him deeply. As a schoolboy he had once been required to write about the ideal horse, which, at the mere
sight of his master's whip, would act obediently. Writing
the composition, Lafayette had described the ideal horse

as one which, upon seeing the whip, promptly threw its master.

La Victoire wallowed on. Slow as a turtle and helpless in her arms, a pair of rusty cannon, she posed an inviting target. Her enemies were both the British men-of-war and the French with royal orders to halt her. But land was reached safely. On Friday, June 13, 1777, she put into North Inlet, South Carolina. Setting foot on shore, the jubilant Lafayette vowed to defend the American cause or perish, and the hindmost to the King who wanted to keep Frenchmen out of somebody else's war.

He had landed at the wrong spot, however. Charleston, his immediate destination, was fifty miles south. The knight-errant was undaunted. Procuring three mounts, he took one of his two valets and a fellow major general, Baron de Kalb. They rode two days and arrived exhausted. The rest of the party followed on foot and reached the city three days later, swollen by mosquito bites.

Their reception was ungenerous. Charleston was choked by French rogues seeking commissions as generals in the Continental Army. The ragged Marquis and his ragged staff were soundly hooted. When it became known that the Marquis was indeed a marquis and that he had brought his own ship (though not quite his free and clear), the upper classes brushed aside the trivia of prejudice. The foreigners were welcomed with a week of fetes.

For all its hospitality, Charleston was not Philadelphia. To get to the capital, Lafayette needed funds. *La Victoire* and her cargo, intended to provide the money, was not completely his, the captain inconsiderately reminded him, and not yet for sale. The youth borrowed seven thousand dollars on his personal note. *La Victoire* sailed for Bordeaux, hit a bar in Charleston Harbor, and sank. Lafayette sped out of Charleston in a handsome new barouche while the people cheered him to the skies.

Thirty-two days later the Marquis and his party rode (the barouche had fallen apart) into Philadelphia. They had their letters of recommendation conveyed to the President of the Congress while they waited out in the street. Instead of President Hancock, they got James Lovell, chairman of the Committee on Foreign Relations. Lovell's French was good, and his method of cutting down French soldiers of fortune was superb. The American army, he told the bedraggled group, had need of officers last year, not this. Messieurs, adieu.

The Marquis dashed off a letter to John Hancock. "After the sacrifices I have made," he wrote, "I have the right to demand two favors. The first is to serve at my own expense. The second is to begin my service as a volunteer."

The beguiling offer won him the attention of Hancock and the scarf of a major general, though no command. The next evening he met Washington.

Something happened in the crowded parlor. Many pressed about Washington. Yet only in one, the awed boy from overseas, did the lordly Virginian find a spirit new and exciting. A chord of enchantment trembled between them. One of those rare lifetime friendships was struck almost on sight.

Washington was forty-nine, the towering leader of a nation. Lafayette was unbelievably young, a boy general who had yet to tread a battlefield. He was tall and thin, timid and chivalrous. He spoke English haltingly. He shone, and he captivated the grave Washington completely.

The next day he accompanied the Commander in Chief on a tour of the fortifications along the Delaware. Thereafter he was treated like a son. His position as a volunteer on Washington's staff embarrassed French diplomats, who were trying to assure Great Britain of the neutrality of France.

He teased Washington for troops of his own. On September 11, at Brandywine, he had the good fortune to be slightly wounded. The wound, bravely borne, earned him the acceptance of the men and the command of a division of Virginians.

During the winter at Valley Forge he was detached to carry out a fantastic, unrealized invasion of Canada at the head of a tiny army. The conquest of Canada, never fulfilled, was Lafayette's persistent darling. He dreamed of retaking the French provinces and handing them over to the Americans in the grandest gesture ever transacted among the nations of the earth.

In January, 1779, he returned to France on furlough, outfitted with the expectation of the elegant sword voted by Congress and a letter to King Louis XVI lauding him to the skies. He plunged joyously into rounds of kisses, toasts, entertainments. While the rage of Paris, he was plotting another blow against England: an invasion of the Isle in consort with Spain. The invasion force, however, dawdled and dispersed. France entered the Revolution. Lafayette fought back tears when the King passed him over and gave the command of the expeditionary force to Rochambeau. Having christened his son Georges Washington, he sailed for America.

He aided liaison between the French and Continental officers. He snapped at Cornwallis "like a terrier baiting a bull" as the British general backed into the dead end at Yorktown. He returned to France in 1781, an idol in two countries.

During the Revolution the boy prodigy had distinguished himself as unofficial ambassador of France. If his contribution as a soldier was flashy and minor, his bond with Washington was exquisite. "Whenever I quit you," he wrote, "I meet with some disappointment and misfortune."

In France his lance was bent, for the field of liberty was cluttered. He jousted through the French Revolution, the reign of Napoleon, and the Bourbon Restoration championing the cause of the downtrodden.

Although he made a triumphal return to America as an old man in 1824-1825, he lives in the United States as the sublime boy of twenty. His was the last hour of chivalry. A simple craving for glory fused with a desire to slay the dragon of tyranny. He sallied forth exactly when Americans and Frenchmen needed a crusader of fair heart.

JOHN BURGOYNE

Curtain at Saratoga

THE SCRIPT FOR THE INVASION OF AMERICA FROM CANADA contained all the essentials of superb drama.

There was the cast of countless thousands: British, Tories, Germans, and redskins, not to mention villainous rebels. The primeval setting of sparkling lakes and mountains painted with the full brush of summer guaranteed unmatched pageantry. The plot unraveled smoothly from a three-way tangle of suspense and timing. The curtain rang down on a happy ending as New England was snuffed from the war.

The author of his untried masterpiece was General John Burgoyne, "the friend to soldiers" and known to one and all as Gentleman Johnny, man-about-town. Burgoyne wielded pen and pistol with equal dexterity. His script, bearing the title *Thoughts on Conducting the War from the Side of Canada*, was presented to the King in November, 1776. Since *Thoughts* closely worded the Cabinet's plans for the 1777 campaign, it was in large measure adopted.

BORN: 1732, Mayfair, England
DIED: August 4, 1792, London, England

As yet the war in America, to which Burgoyne had gone in company with Howe and Clinton, had offered him no spot in the limelight, his favorite illumination. His *Thoughts* promised a change. He had earned one. His military record was fashionably correct. During the Seven Years' War he had developed the cavalry in Portugal. The King had selected "Burgoyne's Light Horse" as a pet and delighted in reviewing it.

As an occasional playwright, Burgoyne enjoyed the friendship of David Garrick, England's foremost actor. In 1774, Garrick had sharpened up one of Burgoyne's amateur theatricals, *The Maid of the Oaks*, and staged it at Drury Lane to modest acclaim. During the siege of Boston, Burgoyne had relieved the gloom with a farce called *The Blockade of Boston* (the Americans had fought back with *The Blockheads*). By way of duty, he had composed Gage's orders in a style so flowery that many a hardened sergeant was seen to reel back slack-jawed after one whiff.

On paper the invasion of America from Canada looked like a smash success. (What commander ever failed on paper?) Reduced to simplest form, the plan called for a three-pronged attack.

A main army of British, Tories, Germans, and Indians, led by Gentleman Johnny himself, was to step off from Canada and proceed south down the tried and true invasion route along the Lake Champlain–Hudson River corridor to Albany. A similar but smaller army under Lieutenant Colonel Barry St. Leger was to descend from its Lake Ontario base and push eastward along the Mohawk Valley to rendezvous with Burgoyne on the steep streets of Albany. The combined northern columns were to act as an anvil for the blow Sir William Howe was to strike with a powerful force sent up the Hudson from New York.

The drama met casting problems right at the start. General Howe, one of the stars, sent word that he would not play the hammer. At least, he would not ship troops from New York unless Washington headed from the Hudson Highlands to meet the invasion.

Moreover, only one hundred Tories leaped to arms. The number of Indians, about four hundred, was disappointing, too. England shook with protests over the use of savages (who would provide more disgrace than help).

Burgoyne cautioned his redskinned auxiliaries in a lofty speech that put a crimp in the jaw of the translator. He positively forbade "bloodshed when you are not opposed in arms." The Indians grunted (or did they chortle?), downed their allotment of rum, and threw themselves into a war dance.

On the morning of July 1, 1777, the expedition sailed from Cumberland Head. Burgoyne had inveigled the command from the King, leapfrogging Britain's chief in Canada, Sir Guy Carleton. The mile-long flotilla of sloops, barges, bateaux, and war canoes carried seventy-five hundred men, an unnecessary load of 138 guns, and uncounted female camp followers. Included in the petticoat battalions was Gentleman Johnny's new favorite, Madame Rousseau, the adorable wife of one of his commissaries.

The opening scenes passed without miscue. Burgoyne issued a high-flown General Order that "This Army Must Not Retreat." The rebel garrison evacuated Fort Ticonderoga and scattered before his hard-fighting advance corps.

Rebel resistance was merely scattered, not demolished, however. It began to rumble louder and louder in the wings. Gentleman Johnny listened not.

He was occupied in Skenesborough at the home of the proprietor, Philip Skene. Until his advance corps returned, he took comfort in his portmanteaus, his ditty bags, his rug rolls, and his lady friend. He glowed with the satisfaction of a playwright whose first act promises a successful run.

All that remained was the water passage down Lake George to the Hudson and thence downriver to Albany and the glorious junction with St. Leger, the route proposed in his *Thoughts*.

But now the dashing playwright decided to edit. He improvised an overland route through twenty miles of forest and swamps. The original route, he contended, meant a backward movement to Fort Ticonderoga and might depress his men by its illusion of retreat. Also, his host could not be slighted.

Philip Skene was a former British army major. He had founded Skenesborough, and it would be a fine thing to have his colony connected to the Hudson. It took Burgoyne's soldiers twenty precious days to cut and thrash and build through those twenty miles. Mine host Skene got his road—and forty bridges, one of them two miles long, in the bargain.

On July 29, Gentleman Johnny broke out of the wilderness and settled himself and his varied comforts in the old Smythe house. The dash to Albany was postponed while his artillery was hauled over the makeshift road. Since no entrenched enemy position lay ahead, so much artillery was a delaying nuisance. But the memory of the Americans dug in at Bunker Hill cast a long shadow. . . .

On August 3, the drama stumbled fearfully. Into camp came a letter from Sir William Howe. It advised Burgoyne that he was going into Pennsylvania. (Lord Germain's bobbled order that Howe cooperate with Burgoyne was not to reach Sir Billy in time.) Howe wished Gentleman Johnny and his troupe all success.

From then on, Burgoyne's cast began to disappear off stage and on. The temptation to gather in rebel stores and recruit Tories cost him eight hundred Germans at Bennington. A week later the curtain jarred down on Act Two with the news of the debacle at Fort Stanwix. St. Leger would not join him at Albany or anywhere else.

Suddenly Gentleman Johnny stood alone on the stage. "This army must not retreat," he repeated.

He loitered until September, hoping for reinforcements from Clinton in New York. By September 19 his dwindling provisions dictated action. He engaged the enemy, was checked at Freeman's Farm, and given a bad case of the jitters. Two weeks more of stalling and dickering and he realized that Clinton too had forsaken him. Something went out of General John Burgoyne.

Like an actor who has forgotten both his lines and the plot, he deployed his men recklessly at the second Battle of Freeman's Farm. Smashed by Arnold and Morgan, he limped to the heights of Saratoga.

The final act of the tragedy was finished. Fate had predestined against him, decreeing that the order to Howe to cooperate should be mishandled in England. Burgoyne's personal conflict—his impulsiveness versus his sense of duty—had crippled the expedition and allowed his enemies time to gather strength. Encircled by a force three times as large as his own, he surrendered his entire army.

Gentleman Johnny departed the American scene in style, wined and dined and fawned upon by Generals Gates, Heath, Schuyler, and Glover. In England he bowed to the lonely applause of his wife, for the Cabinet asked no encores of a loser. A few harmless titles, like scentless bouquets, were bestowed: Commander in Chief in Ireland, Muster-Master General for Foreign Forces in Canada, etc.

His sword rusted but his pen flourished. His comedy, *The Heiress*, appeared in 1786 and attained genuine success.

Playwright, then, or general?

Here is the puzzle. It has never been the function of a general to write plays or a playwright to conduct war.

The final judgment rests with the silent men who did not cheer *The Heiress*. Some had passed bit by bit through the bellies of wolves and some had rotted three and four to a grave along the route of Gentleman Johnny's extravaganza from Cumberland Head to Saratoga.

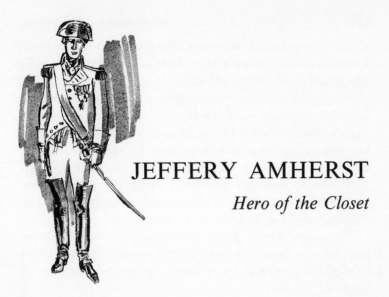

JEFFERY AMHERST

Hero of the Closet

WITH BURGOYNE'S ARMY IN THE HANDS OF CONGRESS AND Howe camped aimlessly in Philadelphia, George III summoned the one man who he believed could scoop victory from the shambles in America.

That man was Jeffery Amherst. His name had once rung in accents great across the width and breadth of England. It was Amherst who had masterminded Britain's North American campaign during the Seven Years' War. It was Amherst who had chilled the French commander of Montreal with the ultimatum, "I have come to take Canada, and I will take nothing else." And Canada he had taken.

A loyal soldier of the King for forty-three of his sixty-one years, Amherst heeded promptly this new call to arms. In front of St. James he stepped gravely out of his carriage— and out of the obscurity of the last fifteen years—a tall, thin figure, erect and forbidding, his once unblemished

BORN: January 29, 1717, Riverhead, England
DIED: August 3, 1797, "Montreal," England

auburn locks dashed with gray. The wart on his left cheek, a deformity in a lesser man, somehow heightened the distinguished aspect of the old hero.

He wore again his crimson dress uniform. On his chest the Star of the Order of the Bath flashed twice in the four o'clock sun. If he suspected that the King's "important announcement" was a charge that he reconquer North America, his sharp features betrayed no hint of his feelings.

He passed through the green reception room walled with heavy tapestries and entered the anteroom, or "closet," and the presence of his King.

The appointment fell from the King's thick, sluggish lips. Amherst was to be once more Commander in Chief of His Majesty's Forces in America, once more the man of the hour.

Amherst bowed at the honor. Courteously, firmly, he refused it.

The thick lips quivered in astonishment. What? Had not Amherst himself declared after the Seven Years' War that an army of seventy-five hundred, apart from artillerymen, could guard against disobedience of the colonies, and, in the bargain, restrain the French, Spanish, and Indians? A decade later, was not Amherst declaring that with five thousand men he could parade unchallenged from Montreal to Georgia?

True, Amherst had said these things. Times had changed, however. The Americans' will to be free had transformed them into an immeasurable foe. By comparison, the greed of France and Spain for new lands and trade was rickety decadence; the lustings of the redskins for rum, scalps, and livestock were the games of primitives. To crush the spirit of freedom, the English must send forty thousand soldiers. Such a force was clearly impossible to recruit, transport, and maintain, Amherst knew.

He had often spoken of the alternative. A blockade.

Funnel all energies into the navy. Strangle American commerce. Sink American shipping.

The King would have nothing to do with talk that suggested timidity. Stunned, vexed, he slid into the skittish manner of speaking peculiar to his strange, foreboding moods of excitement. He poured out a deluge of questions to which he gave the answers hippity-hoppity.

Was Sir Jeffery free of blame for the comedy in America? No! Hadn't he declined the position of Commander in Chief once before? Yes! Whom had he approved in his stead? *Three* generals—Howe, Burgoyne, and Clinton! The King paused, blowing out his cheeks. His prominent eyes stared almost pleadingly. An air of bygone greatness seemed to swell from the silent, inflexible old conqueror opposite him, billowing the name *Amherst* like a remote zephyr of hope.

Amherst, who fifteen years ago had marched through a foreign wilderness for more than a thousand miles and converged three armies on schedule before Montreal . . . *Amherst*, to whom even the splendid James Wolfe had been subordinate . . . *Amherst*, who had compelled the surrender of sixteen French battalions . . . *Amherst*, who had affixed to the Empire a domain a dozen times larger than the motherland.

In the King's time, only Lord Clive in India had rivaled Amherst's success. Clive was dead, a suicide in 1774. And here was faithful Amherst, the man most fitted by experience and skill to chasten the rebels, obstinately refusing to take the field.

George III clenched his puffy fists and charged from the room. The interview was over.

Back home to Kent went Jeffery Amherst. Home was his beloved brick mansion "Montreal." How he had yearned for the English countryside while tramping through the limitless American forests! "I have no thought of returning to America," he had written when long after victory the King had finally permitted him to quit the scene.

His homecoming had been shorn of the honors due the first citizen of the New World. Nations at peace forget the heroes of war. His arrival in London three years after the winning of Canada created no more of a stir than if he had been a molasses salesman. His patron, William Pitt the Elder, was prime minister no longer. His Majesty had enough worries without giving the populace an idol to adore above himself. Even in his private life, Amherst had found emptiness. His wife, who had opposed his going to the colonies, had grown fatally insane during his five-year absence.

Once he had written her that wherever the King cared to send him, "I shall very gladly go." But in a second interview with George III, Amherst again declined to direct the impossible task in America. The refusal took colossal courage. George III revered his kingship; whoever disagreed with him was a "traitor or a scoundrel."

Two months later, on March 13, 1778, the war leaped to England's doorstep. The French ambassador notified the secretary of state that King Louis XVI had signed an alliance with the United States of America. Britain's number one soldier hastened from "Montreal" to accept the appointment of Commander in Chief of the home army.

His paramount concern lay in the immediate fashioning of a defense against invasion. (One of his European scouts reported that a hundred thousand French troops perched on the Normandy coast ready to embark.) Despite the tremendous pressure of an alarmed Parliament and a terrified citizenry, the veteran stayed calm, steady, and constant.

Trained manpower was scarce. England's small regular army speckled the globe—fighting in the colonies, guarding

Canada and the West Indies, occupying Gibraltar and the posts in India. Amherst designated area military officers throughout the kingdom and set them to training militia. He put his engineers to repairing highways. He wanted his forces to balance by mobility what they lacked in heft.

In April, 1779, Spain allied with France. During that critical summer, Amherst juggled his guardsmen back and forth across the nation, as much for defense as to confound enemy spies about any vulnerable spot on the coast. A city might be garrisoned one week by two thousand men and a month later by twelve thousand. So the remaining years of the Revolution witnessed an odd double image. While the Americans fought for their rights and property across the Atlantic, Englishmen prepared to do exactly the same.

Early in the morning of August 19, 1779, the sails of a French fleet cut the horizon off Plymouth. The enemy armada, however, was impaired by the failure of the inept Spanish squadrons to participate, and by an epidemic which decimated the French crews. The gallant appearance of British ships and a battering storm delivered the coup de grace. The invasion was abandoned, permanently.

Unaware of the enemy's decision, Amherst never relaxed his vigilance till the conclusion of hostilities. On the internal front he smoothened the endless squabbles among his amateur soldiers. He controlled London during the Gordon Riots. He guided Burgoyne clear of disgrace and approved Cornwallis for an American command.

To his distaste the rank of Commander in Chief seated him in the Cabinet. Mistrustful of politics, often the victim of politicians, he refrained from voicing opinions. He simply voted "yes" or "no" on a subject.

Except for brief intervals, he served as Commander in Chief for the duration of his public life. In America his name is commemorated by Amherst College in Massachusetts. In England he reigns as the greatest general between Marlborough and Wellington.

A softly mocking air hovers over the idealized paintings of the British generals who got stuck with the American Revolution. Amherst gazes from his portraits untainted. Wise and brave, he was never wiser or braver than when he refused the royal order to command against the rebels.

He died a field marshal.

FREDERICK VON STEUBEN
Drill Master

One of Benjamin Franklin's most successful inventions was General Frederick von Steuben.

Von Steuben was an authentic baron but no more than a former captain in the Prussian army, when, a trifle frayed at the cuffs, he presented himself to Franklin in Paris. The wise old statesman appraised the penniless job hunter, taking heed of the backing accorded him by Count de St. Germain, French minister of war. Franklin decided that the Baron, with some dressing up, was what the struggling Continental Army needed badly—a competent technical adviser.

Franklin scratched out a letter that doubled as a recommendation to Congress and a birth certificate. It created the most imposing foreign volunteer of the war—Lieutenant General von Steuben, lately of the staff of Frederick the Great of Prussia.

The meteoric ascent from captain to lieutenant general unsteadied Von Steuben not one tremor. At forty-six he

Born: September 17, 1730, Magdeburg, Prussia
Died: November 28, 1794, Mohawk country, N.Y.

was nicely practiced in the art of reworking his personal history for the best shine.

With money in his pocket, Von Steuben collected a personal staff befitting his heady rank. Uniforms were purchased of scarlet regimentals turned up with blue, for he had been misadvised that the Americans had adopted the colors of the British army. Over his heart he pinned a star-shaped medal as big as a saucepan.

His party boarded ship for America in the winter of 1777, having among its number but one who was not an impersonator. This was Azor, an Italian greyhound that ate for two.

In America, Von Steuben was coached on recent military and political affairs by Robert Morris and Franklin's son-in-law, Richard Bache, who had been taken into the conspiracy. Negotiating with Congress, the "lieutenant-general" bore himself with charming modesty. His demands were reasonable. If the Revolution was successful, he expected to be rewarded in keeping with his contribution.

Benjamin Franklin had fashioned well. Von Steuben's modesty, his rank, and his experience in the Prussian army, the hallowed military school of the civilized world, impressed Congress. The resolve not to hire any more foreigners was waived. General Von Steuben was sent to join the main army at its winter quarters in Valley Forge.

By now he and his staff had put right the error of their attire with Continental blue and buff. It is a good bet that Von Steuben did not buy a new uniform, but had his scarlet one dyed. Although a disciplined soldier, he never developed into a disciplined man. In America as in Europe, he was always short of ready money.

Having been steered toward fame by others, the impostor had to travel the rest of the road on his own. He nurtured no misgivings. He had learned his profession with German thoroughness. He knew what made an army hard and proud.

During the Seven Years' War he had compiled a notable record. Afterward, he had been one of thirteen handpicked pupils in a special military class taught personally by Frederick the Great. But the peacetime cutback of the Prussian army had set him adrift.

He had floated about the courts of Europe for fourteen years, selling his sword after the custom of the day. If he hadn't exactly been the right-hand man of Frederick the Great, he was in truth the good friend of the King's brother, Prince Henry.

The Star of the Order of Fidelity, the huge medal that never forsook his breast, was awarded him when he was chamberlain at a petty court. To qualify, he had rewritten his family tree, a work started by his grandfather. Von Steuben millers and Von Steuben tenant farmers were dubbed princelings with a touch of the Von Steuben pen.

He sprayed his deception without favoritism. If he misrepresented his life in Europe to the Americans, he constantly misled his German friends about his bountiful and glamorous life in America. Of his reception at Valley Forge he wrote to Chancellor Frank of Hechengen:

"General Washington came several miles to meet me on the road, and accompanied me to my quarters, where I found an officer with twenty-five men as guard of honor. . . . On the following day the army was mustered, and General Washington accompanied me to review it."

In reality, Washington's reception was courteous but extremely limited. His soldiers kept to their huts, distressed by the cold weather and insufficient food and clothing. Not so much as an undermanned regiment could have been smartened up in time for a review.

Washington accepted Von Steuben's voluntary services with discreet indifference to credentials. The Commander in Chief had been prevented by administrative duties from personally seeing to training. And none of the American-born generals had the technical know-how.

Von Steuben agreed to be acting inspector general, a
title that carried no commission. After a few days of nosing
about Valley Forge, he reported to Washington: no
European army had ever held together under such hardships. Here five hundred horses were to starve to death, and
here nearly twenty-five hundred men were to perish of
sickness and exposure. Infantry drill was scant (though
over in the artillery camps, Henry Knox was whipping
his men into shape). Each unit had its own drill models—
some French, some Prussian, and some English. The
officers, like their English counterparts, were too dignified
to conduct drills, and the ranks contained no competent
drill sergeants.

Von Steuben started from scratch. He dictated instructions at night for immediate translation, and the next day
had them executed on the drill grounds. He formed a
model company of a hundred willing learners and put them
through their paces himself.

The spectacle of a lieutenant general acting as a drill
master soon had the whole army crowding around. Since
he spoke little English, he taught mainly by example: the
manual of arms, how to fix bayonets and charge, how to
load and fire, how to care for equipment, and how to
march in compact masses instead of the damaging strung-
out style the army had been using.

He borrowed from both French and Prussian systems and
streamlined them to meet the needs of his pupils. Un-
essential words, motions, and commands were eliminated.

The American soldier grew on him slowly. To an old
comrade-in-arms he wrote: "You say to your soldier, 'Do
this,' and he does it, but I am obliged to say, 'This is the
reason why you ought to do it,' and then he does it."

The German delighted the Americans with his sense of
humor, his pantomime, and his picturesque flights of
wrath. He had memorized the English commands for the
movements, but when a maneuver miscarried, he grew red

of face and sputtered out a series of oaths in French and
then in German. Whenever he used up his foreign oaths, he
pleaded with an interpreter to curse for him in English.

He drilled the army by squads, companies, battalions,
and finally regiments. By April, five weeks after his arrival,
he had the whole army wheeling and snapping like Europe's
finest. In May, Washington no longer had to play the game
of referring to him as a "lieutenant-general in foreign
service." He became Major General von Steuben, Inspector
General.

During the winter at Valley Forge and afterward,
Steuben wrote his *Regulations for the Order and Discipline of
the Troops of the United States*, popularly known as the "blue
book." It became the military bible of the army. Throughout the war he tightened the army organization. He enjoyed
an occasional field command in the south, but it is as a
teacher that he made his vital contribution.

His training methods at Valley Forge not only prepared
the army for the coming campaign but molded a cadre
that rapidly absorbed each year's recruits. Never again did
the rebels fly from bayonets as at Bunker Hill. Indeed, they
captured Stony Point almost exclusively by bayonet.

Congress liberally rewarded Von Steuben after the war
with money and lands. He continued to hunt greater riches
around the corner and lost heavily in speculations. A
bachelor, he lived his last years in New York City and in
Steuben Manor, a log cabin in the Mohawk wilderness,
where he died.

He has been called indispensable, and perhaps he was.
He took an army of privates who were all generals, and
none soldiers, and taught them everything they had to
know to win.

The Prussian captain could not have done more had
his rank of lieutenant general in the Prussian army been
genuine.

WILLIAM PITT
The Unfinished Speech

ON A DAY WHEN THE REVOLUTION WAS THREE YEARS OLD the Duke of Richmond received an extraordinary message. It hinted that a way to resolve the war would be presented before the House of Lords.

The date was April 6, 1778. A shroud of dejection had covered Parliament since the disaster at Saratoga the previous October. The Opposition was stepping up its pressure for a halt to the fighting. Richmond led the way, convinced of the "improbability of compelling America to subjection by war."

He planned to introduce on the following day a motion urging the King to dismiss his ministers and to recall his troops from America. Hoping for support for his program, he had written to England's foremost statesman, William Pitt, once the Great Commoner and since his "fall up-stairs" the Earl of Chatham.

Too sick to reply by his own hand, Pitt had dictated his

BORN: November 15, 1708, London, England
DIED: May 11, 1778, Hayes, England

answer. The seventy-year-old statesman made it clear that he stood not for Richmond's program of sovereignty for America, but for America's allegiance to the Throne. He would, the message read, quit the comfort of his country estate and himself seek an honorable conclusion to the war.

Richmond was overjoyed. He foresaw a solution more gracious to England than his own abject surrender. The great Pitt was forsaking the cozy shadows of his hearthstone to flash again the lightning of his mind. The genius who built the Empire was coming to save it.

On the fateful April Tuesday the wigged, crimson-robed lords filed into their long chamber. Few were aware of Pitt's promised appearance. Not even the excited Richmond suspected that he would shortly behold the most dramatic hour in the history of Parliament.

As the peers took their places on the double rows of facing benches, a commotion arose in the corridor. In a moment Pitt entered, held up on one side by his son-in-law, Lord Mahon, and on the other by his son William, who was to walk in his footsteps.

He advanced laboriously, working his crutches, an apparition from the heroic past. His hawklike face with its huge Roman nose, penetrating black eyes, and mobile mouth gleamed palely beneath the thick wig. He wore not the red robe of a lord. A mantle of flannel swathed him to the knees, obscuring the black velvet suit that had distinguished him in the House of Commons. There long ago he had spoken against the Stamp Act. "I rejoice that America has resisted," he had proclaimed. Steadfastly he had supported the rights of the colonials as he had the rights of all Englishmen.

As he progressed toward the front of the chamber, the entire House rose in silent tribute to its noblest member. He took his place and nodded. Mahon and William withdrew, and the assembly sat.

The Duke of Richmond, according to plan, made his motion to dismiss the ministers and to remove the troops from America. Lord Weymouth countered for the government. When Weymouth finished, Pitt pulled himself slowly to his feet and adjusted his crutches.

The black eyes "which would cut a diamond" swept the room. They fixed briefly upon one of the wall tapestries that depicted the defeat of the Spanish Armada. The parchmentlike lids closed, as if Pitt were thinking back twenty-two years when he had taken hold of the nation during another crisis.

"I know I can save this country, and that no one else can," he had said. He had leveled party differences, hand-picked generals and admirals, and called upon the people to build ships and to sail them. He had distracted France with hit-and-run raids. When the Seven Years' War was done, Britain controlled North America and India; she had reoccupied her Mediterranean base of Minorca and had expanded her territories in the West Indies and Africa. Most vital of all, William Pitt had restored England's confidence to move ahead on her own.

Now the lords of England sat expectantly, every gaze trained on the singular, emaciated figure enveloped in the folds of flannel. The imperious lips that had once released the most brilliant oratory in the English language quivered and parted, the eyes opened toward heaven.

"I thank God that He has enabled me to come this day to do my duty . . ."

The faint, quavering voice paused to gather strength.

"My lords, I rejoice that the grave has not closed upon me, that I am still alive to lift up my voice against the dismemberment of this ancient and most noble monarchy. Pressed down as I am by the hand of infirmity, I am little able to assist my country in this most perilous conjuncture. But, my lords, while I have sense and memory, I will never consent to deprive the royal offspring of the House of

Brunswick, the heirs of the Princess Sophia, of their fairest inheritance. Where is the man that will dare to advise such a measure?"

The long white hands, coached by the actor David Garrick to express disdain or amusement with the subtlest flexion, uncurled from the crutches.

"Surely, my lords, this nation is no longer what it was! Shall a people that seventeen years ago was the terror of the world, now stoop so low as to tell its ancient inveterate enemy, *take all we have only give us peace?* It is impossible!

"I wage war with no men. I wish for none of their employments; nor would I cooperate with men who still persist in unretracted error, or who, instead of acting on a firm decisive line of conduct, halt between two opinions, where there is a middle path.

"In God's name, if it is absolutely necessary to declare either for peace or war, and the former cannot be restored with honor, why is not the latter commenced without hesitation? I am not, I confess, well informed of the resources of this kingdom, but I trust it has still sufficient to maintain its just rights, though I know them not. But my lords, any state is better than despair."

The man was lost in the voice. The magical tones swelled.

"Let us at least make one effort; and if we must fall, let us fall like men!"

The mass of flannel drapes lowered onto the bench. Richmond looked stunned. The other lords remained silent, profoundly stirred by this eloquence from a bygone age. But Richmond's silence was born of shock, not admiration.

Pitt's words were a *battle cry!* Where was the solution at which he had hinted?

Richmond collected himself, rose, and after courteously conceding Pitt's past contributions, recited the calamitous condition of the country. Pitt listened attentively. When Richmond concluded, he again struggled to his feet.

He was flushed and obviously agitated. Suddenly he swayed, passed a hand to his heart, and toppled backward.

The entire House was thrown into confusion. Lord Mansfield alone kept his seat, watching with macabre interest the seeming death throes of his inveterate foe. The others hurried about frantically, some chasing after help, some producing salts and spirits, some crowding around the fragile figure.

Pitt was borne to his country house at Hayes in Kent, where he lingered for several weeks. He died on May 11, 1778, his last speech clotted in his throat.

Had he planned to divulge some solution? Was his speech designed in two parts—one of those brilliant stratagems of oratory for which he was celebrated?

In former days he had advised that Congress be recognized within a liberal British Empire. Did he propose to reiterate his lifelong goal of a far-flung empire of freemen, backed by his willingness to administer such a polity? For Pitt and Pitt alone had the chance, if any chance existed, of peaceably repairing the cracks in the New World.

His personal prestige in America was enormous. Statuettes and pictures of him bedecked countless American parlors. South Carolina had voted to erect a statue of him in Charleston. Benjamin Franklin had been his counselor on affairs of the colonies before the war, and each man held the other in highest esteem and trust.

Did Pitt really have a solution, or did he say his all? Had he risen that second time to refute Richmond's motion to end the war only to break under the awful truth that the day of reconciliation had passed? Had he died after bequeathing England but a rallying cry to fight on?

"I can't help observing," wrote Sir Joseph Yorke, "that he made us too great at too great an expense to leave us in the lurch . . ."

BENJAMIN TALLMADGE

Birth of the Secret Service

IT WAS NOT A PLAYFUL EXAMINATION. NAPHTALI DAGGETT, acting president of Yale College, sat on one side of the heavy oak desk in the den of the Reverend Benjamin Tallmadge. Opposite him sat the minister's bright-eyed little son, Ben, age twelve.

The snowy-haired educator questioned the jot of a boy in all corners of classical learning. At the conclusion of an hour, Daggett rose and pronounced to his host, "Your son is qualified to enter Yale."

The Reverend Mr. Tallmadge was pleased but unsurprised. He had put Ben, his keenest son, in a class with several boys whom he was preparing for college. Although Ben sponged up knowledge at a swipe, he was in other ways immature. His father kept him home three years.

In the autumn of 1769, Ben Tallmadge went to Yale. As he could pass without the toil of study, he compiled a lusterless record, though he participated in the highlight

BORN: February 25, 1754, Brookhaven, N.Y.
DIED: March 7, 1835, Litchfield, Conn.

of the commencement program. With his close chum Nathan Hale and two other youths he debated the tantalizing subject, "Whether the Education of Daughters be not, without any just reason, more neglected than that of sons."

By now Benjamin Tallmadge was above average height, big enough to make his own decisions about his future. He accepted the post of schoolmaster at the high school in Weathersfield, Connecticut.

When war started, he refused to rush unthinkingly to arms. With a few friends he rode to Cambridge in June, 1775, to take stock of the opposing sides. What he saw fired him with the ardor to enlist in the rebel army, and with the urge to compose a poem.

The poem he composed immediately. The ardor to enlist burned with a low, cautious flame till a favorable wind blew his way. In the spring John Chester, a fellow townsman, was named colonel of the Connecticut State Regiment. Benjamin Tallmadge walked in as adjutant with the rank of lieutenant.

Before his commission became official, the underpaid schoolmaster stood up at a town meeting. He protested the inadequate clothing of the local soldiers. He marched with his regiment to New York wearing a fine uniform paid for at public expense.

The uniform gave notice that Benjamin Tallmadge could get things done through a rare sense of timing and an artful tongue. He would blend patriotism, egoism, and an uncommon mentality during his years as an officer. In consequence, he would serve well his country and himself.

Within a year Tallmadge had risen to major of the Second Regiment of Continental Light Dragoons. He fought in the battles of Long Island, White Plains, and Brandywine. His tidy capture and destruction of Fort St. George, a Tory supply depot on Long Island, demonstrated his fitness for independent command.

Although he once lost all his papers and baggage to the enemy, Tallmadge earned Washington's respect and confidence. The Commander in Chief even modified his edict that "no stallions, mares, white or grey horses" be purchased for the cavalry in order that Tallmadge could mount his metal-helmeted troops on sturdy dapple-grays.

Between 1776 and 1778 Tallmadge and his men busily patroled the "neutral ground" between the enemy camps. Here warfare was primitive, bloody, and unchronicled. Saddles and sabers clashed far from the conscience of headquarters, on fields and in woods forgotten by the code of nations. No quarter was asked, and none was given.

Patrol duty, perforce, comprised the main function of the cavalrymen. The sparsity of mounted troops prevented them from being a decisive factor in battle. Now and again because of their advance position, they picked up information on enemy troop movements.

The American system of intelligence was haphazard. Before the summer of 1778, the army had no organized secret service. Each commander depended on his advance units and upon paid spies. The latter were held in low esteem. Their loyalty jumped to the clink of coins. "Few men," Washington declared on the subject of spies, "have the virtue to withstand the highest bidder."

By July, 1778, Washington felt the pressing need for a reliable chain of military intelligence. He assigned the task to Brigadier General Charles Scott, who commanded the advance patrols in Westchester and Fairfield counties. When Scott left the zone in the fall, the work passed to his brainiest subordinate, Major Benjamin Tallmadge.

Tallmadge inherited several dedicated, courageous agents. He fished for others in New York and Long Island. In time he developed a smoothly running organization, a true secret service that provided Washington with ample and accurate information without discovery. It was Tallmadge's alertness to Benedict Arnold's treason that led to the last-second capture of the general's British confederate, Major John André.

In his quest for secrecy, Tallmadge got help from an unusual source. For five or six years Sir James Jay, a physician in England, had been corresponding with his brother, John Jay of New York. They had used an ink, or "stain," of Sir James's concoction. When written on white paper, the ink was invisible till brushed with a developer.

The brothers saw the military possibilities of their ink and placed it at the disposal of General Washington. Delighted, Washington wrote to Colonel Elias Dayton: "Fire which will bring lime juice, milk, and other things of this kind to light, has no effect on it."

The magic fluid was foolproof, or nearly so. The British had secret inks, also. One was developed by heat and a second by a kind of acid. The danger lay in the British growing suspicious of blank pages and finding a developer for the Jay ink.

The spies finally adopted the practice of writing a brief business letter to a known loyalist. The bottom of the sheet contained a message in the invisible ink. If intercepted, the letter created no suspicion. The courier had only to be sure that he delivered the letter to Tallmadge and not to the loyalist.

To go with the invisible ink and fake business letter, Tallmadge added the further precaution of code. He took a dictionary, believed to be Entick's, and numbered the most frequently used words in alphabetical order.

Words beginning with *a* had low numbers: "advice" was 15. Words beginning with letters toward the end of the alphabet had high numbers: "zeal" was 710. Just to be extra safe, he got up a jumbled code of letters so that any word could be composed by his agents.

To complete the whole system he gave prominent places and persons numbers. New York was 727; Long Island, 728; Washington, 711; Tallmadge, 721, and so on.

Tallmadge made only three code books. One copy he kept. One he sent to Washington. The third he entrusted to his ace spy, Robert Townsend, for use of the Long Island agents.

Secret Service work occupied Tallmadge increasingly from 1778 to 1783. He shortened and improved his channels and cooperated with the French under Rochambeau. Withal, he continued in his military duties. When the fighting swung south, the Second Regiment was, as in earlier periods, the only cavalry directly under Washington's command. Tallmadge rode patrol over the neutral ground around New York, suppressing illegal trade and the British partisans.

At the conclusion of the war, British General Sir Guy Carleton warned of a plot to plunder New York and assault any remaining Tories. Since many of his agents posed as Tories, Tallmadge feared for their safety. Upon the withdrawal of the Redcoats, Tallmadge led the Americans into the city in order to protect his men and their property.

The return to civilian life did not catch the former boy wonder with empty pockets. He had, from the first, envied the merchants and their fat army contracts. During winters of relative inactivity, he had cultivated men of influence. With their counsel he had soon begun investing wisely in privateers, discounting bills of exchange, and once, speculating in Connecticut's redemption of paper money.

Establishing himself in Litchfield, Connecticut, he prospered, served eight terms in the United States House of Representatives, and contributed liberally to charity. He died at the ripe old age of eighty-one, leaving from a life otherwise eminently planned one chance monument— the United States Secret Service.

GEORGE ROGERS CLARK

Conqueror of the Northwest

ON FEBRUARY 5, 1779, A BAND OF FRONTIERSMEN PARADED through the town of Kaskaskia near the Mississippi. Below the cabins they came to the stockade walls of the fort. There, by one of the corner blockhouses, they halted, knelt upon the frost-hardened mud, and bowed their heads.

Father Gibault delivered a solemn discourse and gave them all absolution. When the priest was done, the men in buckskin rose to their feet and went swinging off.

Their jauntiness reflected the verve of their leader, a spellbinding young colonel named George Rogers Clark. As Virginia's commander in the west, Clark was sallying forth to recapture Vincennes, a danger spot on the Wabash River. The British, using Vincennes as an advance post, could start Indians on the warpath from Canada to Florida.

Clark divided his force. He sent forty-six men on a large row galley armed by six light guns up the Ohio and Wa-

BORN: November 19, 1752, Albemarle County, Va.
DIED: February 13, 1818, Locust Grove, Ky.

bash. They had orders to wait "ten leagues" below Vincennes to cut off British retreat by water. With the remaining 170, nearly half French volunteers, he began the overland trek to Vincennes, two hundred and forty cold, drenched miles away.

The Illinois country in good weather was among the loveliest in the world. In February, it could be the worst. Contesting Clark's path toward the rich territory south of the Great Lakes were four swollen rivers, flooded prairies, and lowlands ankle-deep in mire.

In the east, winter had wrought its usual stalemate. The main American army camped in snug huts around headquarters at Middlebrook, New Jersey. Officers on furlough amused themselves at Philadelphia while within a distant, gurgling wilderness Clark and his Big Knives prepared to scoop out an inland empire.

Morale had to be wrung out daily. As long as game was seen, Clark allowed his men to shoot freely and feast "like Indians at a war dance." He spared neither himself nor his officers in setting examples, "running as much through the mud and water as any of them."

After eight days the expedition slogged within twenty miles of Vincennes, losing but a trickle of its high spirits. Here began the "drowned lands." The two forks of the Little Wabash had overflowed, interlapping in a single sheet of water that stretched five miles between hills.

Hiding his misgivings, Clark ordered the construction of a large canoe. From among the forests of naked trees jutting above the surface, a suitable stock was felled. Teams labored in shifts to fashion a dugout, the first of several such craft to be made along the way. The men waded across what had been bottomland, using the canoe only as a ferry to cross the two rivers. The horses swam. Three days passed before Clark's feet trod firm ground again.

It drizzled continually. Wet and chilled, the men followed the tall, lean-limbed redhead who flamed in a world awash. He invented games, laughed down the suggestion to retreat, made light of hardships, and drove everyone on.

By the evening of February 17, the little army looked down on the Embarrass River. It, too, overflowed. Every inch of the last nine miles to the Wabash and Vincennes just beyond was swamped.

Clark stood in the shallows that once had been the shore. He felt every eye questioning him. He dared not hesitate. Raising his rifle to his chin, he plunged in up to the armpits. The men followed, the weak clinging to the strong.

The worst still loomed ahead. Provisions had spoiled. Small game had vanished. Buffalo and deer had fled. The dull gray shimmer of floodwaters leveled out on all sides.

Half-starved, the Big Knifes sloshed and staggered deeper and deeper into the enemy's zone. They were now in danger of being surprised themselves. Few of their rifles remained in condition to fire.

To buoy sinking spirits, Clark resorted to a ruse. The men in the lead, the tallest and sturdiest, regularly called back, "Shallow ahead!" The others believed and stumbled on.

Water squished in boots and dragged at clothing and dribbled into eyes and nostrils. For long periods there was nothing but moaning and the liquid tones of rain and water. Water seemed to drip into the very brain, to soak the last dry crevice and cell, to gurgle and splash and ooze and seep. Limbs responded with the ponderous weight of soggy flesh and sodden bones.

Clark paused once to speak seriously with an officer. His tense expression touched off alarm, and he quickly acted to avert panic. He whispered to his officers to imitate him. Mixing powder and water, he blackened his face. With a war whoop, he crashed through the water. The officers aped him obediently. The men gasped in astonishment and "fell in like a flock of sheep." Clark called for a song, and singing swelled down the line that had moments earlier wavered in fear.

The Wabash was crossed in forty-eight terrible hours. Two miles from Vincennes, the Big Knives touched paradise—ten acres of dry land. Those too weak to stand without the support of the water slumped against the ice-crusted shore, fingers clawing into the good earth. They were hauled out by tottering comrades and dragged into the concealment of a grove. Fires were built. From a canoe carrying squaws and children, scouts seized a half quarter of buffalo, along with corn, tallow, and kettles. The buffalo meat was boiled into broth and so multiplied sufficiently to nourish the benumbed men.

Hidden within the grove, Clark could see the town. Several inhabitants, unaware of prying eyes, were out shooting ducks. Scouts reported that his presence was unknown to his implacable foe, British Colonel Henry Hamilton. It was Hamilton's use of the Indian tribes north of the Ohio River that earned him the grisly nickname the "Hair Buyer."

The year before, Clark, a surveyor and woodsman, had conquered most of Hamilton's domain in the northwest, having obtained the backing of Virginia, claimant to the vast territory. Armed with a handful of frontiersmen and a silver tongue, Clark had not only bagged Vincennes, he had captured all the forts used by the British as bases for their Indian raids against Pennsylvania, Virginia, and Kentucky.

Hamilton had counterattacked from his Detroit headquarters. He had ousted the two-man garrison left by Clark at Vincennes. While the Englishman settled there till spring, Clark had decided to gamble everything on the advantage of surprise. He had overcome floods and freezing weather. Now, after eighteen days, he rested within sight of his goal.

His first step was to dispatch a letter to the townspeople.

American sympathizers were instructed to stay indoors. All others were directed to find protection inside Fort Sackville. Knowing Clark's reputation, few joined the British.

The timber walls of Fort Sackville were eleven feet high and stout. Hamilton held his own during the 23d, though unknown to Clark he had only part of his force, fewer than a hundred men. A parley in a church failed in producing terms. The next morning Clark again demanded surrender. Hamilton haughtily answered that he was "not disposed to be awed into action unworthy of British subjects."

Awkwardly for Hamilton five of his Indians—unaware of the Big Knives—returned to the fort carrying American scalps. In full view of the British, Clark had the braves bound, seated on the ground in a ring, and tomahawked.

That night Hamilton surrendered to Clark and the "Republic of Virginia."

By his victory, Clark, at twenty-six, held control of the Illinois country again, a grip he maintained throughout the war. The next year he helped defeat the British at St. Louis. In 1782 he saved the frontier settlements from the Shawnees in one of the last actions of the Revolution.

Lack of money and men, two plaguing shortages, thwarted his plans for subduing Detroit, the British seat in the west. But the old northwest, including Detroit, passed to the Americans at the peace table. If General George Rogers Clark went unnamed in the documents, his influence did not go unminded. The deeds of the young redhead embodied the irresistible spirit of westward expansion, and England conceded the inevitable.

The little battle of Vincennes had staked down the claim of the United States to an area half as large as the thirteen rebelling colonies. Victory was won by a youth who quelled the British with rifles and dripping tomahawks, and who for eighteen days raised man, puny creature that he is, above the might of nature.

BANASTRE TARLETON

The British Attila

"To hell with the law!" exclaimed Banastre Tarleton when he learned of the fighting at Concord and Lexington. "These miserable Americans must be taught their places!"

In the opinion of the twenty-one-year-old cavalry officer the open grave and the prisoner-of-war camp were the ideal "places" for the rebels. He could scarcely wait to put them there.

When Lord Cornwallis prepared to sail with reinforcements for America, Tarleton pulled some strings. On December 24, 1775, the muster roll of the First Dragoon Guards stationed at Norwich listed him as "Absent by King's Leave." He had started toward the port of embarkation and his genesis as "Bloody Tarleton."

Passing through London, he strutted into an old haunt, the Cocoa Tree, a fashionable gambling club in St. James Street. While he sat at the faro table, indulging his "cursed

BORN: August 21, 1754, Liverpool, England
DIED: January 25, 1833, Leintwardine, England

itch to play," the conversation turned to the renegade Englishman, General Charles Lee.

Tarleton's hot blood boiled. In a fit of emotion he leaped to his feet and brandished his saber. As unarmed players scattered hither and yon, he screamed, "With this blade I'll cut off the head of General Lee!"

On the day he sailed to chastise the rebels, Tarleton had been a soldier barely ten months. He had sampled Oxford for two years, devoting more time to the playing fields than to studies. Shifting to law, he had wasted another two years in London before abandoning the pretense of books for the amusements vended at the Cocoa Tree and Drury Lane. In April, 1775, the restless youth had seized the opportunity to purchase a commission as cornet. Although the lowest-ranking officer in the cavalry, a cornet had the rip-roaring duty of carrying the standard. Banastre Tarleton had found his career.

He stepped upon American soil unknown and un-noticed. No record of valor set him apart. Physically, he stood below average height. He appeared merely thickset if scrutiny stopped at the waist. In his legs bulged the portent of uncommon rigor. They swelled with the mus-cularity of a Michelangelo marble.

Sculptured by nature to clasp a horse's back, Tarleton burned with the desire to ride as few men ever rode. He was to show the civilized world a savagery it had not beheld since Gothic horsemen shrieked through the Roman forum.

Up in the saddle, with the enemy in front of him, this son of a Liverpool merchant acquired a reputation that com-pensated for his lack of wealth or titled birth. He feared neither death nor the devil, and both Clinton and Corn-wallis took notice. Before long Tarleton was leading cavalry raids, smiting northern shipping centers and destroying the supplies of the Continental Army. He directed the van-guard that captured General Lee, but despite his gambling-house boast, he spared Lee's head.

Such a spasm of leniency gripped Tarleton less and less often. By the middle of 1779 the sulphur of war had purged him of all weakness (save an invulnerable fondness of feminine company), and at the town of Pound Ridge, New York, he cast the terrible mold that shaped his future operations.

The attack marked Tarleton's first independent command. He galloped from his camp on the Bronx River shortly before midnight of July 1. At daybreak he struck with his two hundred men an enemy force of approximate size. Before his furious charge the rebels fled, and Tarleton pursued with his dragoons. The fugitives were ridden down and slaughtered. While passing through the town, he was fired upon by militiamen, and when his command to desist was not instantly obeyed, he calmly set buildings ablaze. He returned to camp triumphant, having covered sixty-four miles in twenty-three hours.

The sequence of a long, hard ride, a furious charge, a ruthless pursuit, and finally the torch, characterized his combat style thereafter. English newspapers published his official report. For the first time his name was widely circulated at home, where it never again was misspelled "Banister" or "Banestier."

Six months after Pound Ridge the British launched their southern campaign. With the armada of 153 ships that put in near Charleston, South Carolina, was young Banastre Tarleton, risen to lieutenant colonel and commandant of the army's most powerful combat team, the British Legion.

Many of Tarleton's carefully trained horses had suffered horribly during the stormy passage. While the lame and sick animals were thrown overboard, he disembarked his men at Port Royal to gather "from friends and enemies, by money or by force, all the horses belonging to the islands in the neighborhood."

The difficulties Tarleton met in filling the places of his lost horses prompted him to simplify his roundup when later he needed mounts. In Virginia, he stole all the thoroughbreds in Hanover County and slit the throats of colts that might eventually carry the enemy.

A perfectionist, he fused the Legion into a superb corps of cavalry and light infantry. Without his leadership— when he lay sick with malaria and then with yellow fever— it fought disjointedly. Handled by the "British Attila," the Legion was the incomparable weapon with which the incomparable cavalryman taught "these miserable Americans their places."

During the maneuvering for Charleston, he surprised three regiments of American horse, including Pulaski's Legion under Major Paul Vernier. The rebels were overwhelmed. Vernier was sabered after he had surrendered.

The next month Tarleton fell upon Lieutenant Colonel Abraham Buford's regiment at the settlement of Waxhaws on the border between the Carolinas. Tarleton himself sabered the standard-bearer as he lifted the white flag. His green-clad dragoons rode amuck through the cowed rebels who vainly tried to surrender. The infantry finished off any Americans still alive.

From the terror-haunted ground at Waxhaws rose the American battle cry, "Tarleton's Quarter!" But stronger stuff than slogans was needed to withstand the terrifying charges of the Green Dragoon.

Acting as Cornwallis' eyes and doing his dirty work, Tarleton cossacked through the south, burning and scattering resistance. (Often, it should be remarked, he neglected to ascertain the sentiments of his victims.) Twice he cut up the partisan forces of doughty Thomas Sumter. The nettlesome Francis Marion, however, he pursued in raging frustration.

Upon learning that the widow of General Richard Richardson had warned Marion of his approach, Tarleton exacted ghoulish revenge. After dining at her table, he declared that he wished to look upon the face of her brave husband. He had his troops dig the corpse from its grave. Then he licked up the last morsel of vengeance by leaving the plantation in humps of smoking ashes.

The American cavalry had no answer to Tarleton. It took a foot soldier, that roughhewn genius of war, Daniel Morgan, to trap him. Aware of Tarleton's methods of long pursuit and unhesitating charge, Morgan staged a deadly theatrical at Cowpens. He pulled his two front lines back after they had fired. Tarleton mistook the maneuver for retreat. He hurled his tired Legion forward, and Morgan demolished nine tenths of it.

If Cowpens ruined Tarleton's reputation for invincibility, nobody told the Green Dragoon. He rebuilt the Legion and roused his men with the taunt, "Remember Cowpens!" Moving north with Cornwallis, he spread such terror that the "King's troops passed through the most hostile part of North Carolina without a shot from the Militia."

In the costly British victory at Guilford Courthouse, North Carolina, on March 15, 1781, Tarleton received a wound in the right hand. A surgeon amputated his forefinger and middle finger. Undaunted, he continued at the head of the Legion, holding the reins in his left hand, his right in a sling. He charged the enemy without means of protecting himself. By the time Cornwallis retired to Yorktown, he had learned to use pistol and saber with his left hand.

The fall of Yorktown ended the peril of death for all the British except one. Banastre Tarleton, the man the Americans hated most, feared for his life. He obtained the amused protection of Count de Rochambeau, the French commander.

Washington invited Cornwallis to dine. Other Continental officers entertained their British counterparts.

Tarleton was pointedly snubbed by the victorious Americans.

On December 15, 1781, he sailed with other paroled officers for England. His countrymen welcomed him as a national hero. He sat in Parliament, rose to full general, and toyed with the heart of London's most beautiful woman, the actress-authoress Mary Robinson.

Still, he nearly did not get to savor the fruits of valor. His alarm over his assassins was justified. On a night shortly after the Yorktown surrender his French protectors secretly changed his quarters.

The next morning it was discovered that the bed on which he ordinarily slept had been stabbed from head to foot.

CASIMIR PULASKI
Patriot from Poland

Count Casimir Pulaski spun the pistol high into the air. With a yeowing cry he dug back his spurs. Rider and mount whirled in an intricate maneuver that sprayed turf in all directions. The breakneck pattern was completed as Pulaski caught the pistol as it fell past his shoulder.

The American officers applauded the stunt. The youthful Pole grinned. It amused him to perform feats of horsemanship, and such exhibitions filled the hours of waiting. For three weeks he had been hurrying back and forth to Philadelphia, pressing Congress about his commission. The slowness of legislative decision infuriated him; this supremacy of civil authority over the military was utterly baffling. Didn't they know he had come to *fight!*

The opportunity to demonstrate valor arose a week later at the Battle of Brandywine on September 11, 1777. Casimir Pulaski, who had reaped fame on Polish battlefields, rode with Washington's staff as a volunteer aide without com-

Born: March 4, 1748, Winiary, Poland
Died: October 11, 1779, aboard *Wasp*

mission or command. Neither was needed once gunsmoke reached his nostrils.

The American right began to crumble. Pulaski galloped over to General Washington and asked permission to lead the headquarters cavalry of thirty men. The harassed Washington consented. Pulaski formed the little detachment and charged. The surprise thrust caused a moment's delay, a moment precious to the retreating Americans.

Although an American defeat, Brandywine represented a personal triumph for Pulaski. That he was blindly out of step with Revolutionary warfare was not, of course, immediately apparent. The impetuous little charge had marked him a fighting leader, a distinction which all his flaws, once unmasked, never impaired.

Four days later Congress finally acted, naming him brigadier general in command of the cavalry. Washington had originally wished the assignment for Joseph Reed, but Reed had refused it. So Washington approved of Pulaski, who had been pounding all ears at headquarters with tales of his use of horse in Poland.

The tales were genuine. A hero of the Polish uprising, he had resisted the gigantic nibbling of Russia, Austria, and Prussia. He knew about defying kings and foreign domination. For many years the three powerful nations had vied to expand their domains at the expense of Poland. In 1768 Pulaski's father had founded the Confederation of Bar, a Catholic resistance force. In the Confederation's military ranks Casimir swiftly reached the top. He defeated the Russians at the city of Czestochowa, gaining for Polish troops their first victory in nearly a century. He survived defeat after defeat. Ultimately the patriotic movement collapsed in shame from an unsuccessful attempt to kidnap and murder the King, a puppet of Russia.

That Pulaski had a hand in a deed so black as attempted murder is doubtful. Nevertheless, he fled Poland under the

King's sentence: his hands were to be displayed on public roads, his body beheaded and quartered and scattered.

The fallen hero wandered Europe seeking employment in various armies. None would have a "regicide." He spent a month in a French prison for debt. Friends rescued him and related his plight to Benjamin Franklin. The young Pole had perhaps the most glittering reputation of any European suggested for American service. Soon he was crossing the Atlantic with promises of a high command in the Continental Army.

He spoke no English and knew next to nothing about America. The people fought for independence, and that was enough. He fondled grand expectations and grander schemes.

He would prepare an expedition to capture the British island of Madagascar and from there swoop upon British commerce in the Indian Ocean. He would organize a special brigade of discontented European officers and let them perform gallantly in their own traditions. He would establish a chain of forts along the Canadian frontier.

Reality unhorsed him. He started on a par with the American officers. That meant on the ground, wrestling with shortages of money, supplies, and manpower.

His cavalry command was the neglected arm of the service—seven hundred and thirty men in four regiments. Large numbers were forever being detached, making training and reorganization simply impossible. General Pulaski contributed little cover for the American retreat from Germantown, his first battle command before the army repaired to Valley Forge.

To make amends, the young Count tried that winter to train his four regiments as a unit, something which had never been essayed. But Washington was unsympathetic to an independent cavalry; he preferred to think of horse in terms of scouting and reconnaissance.

This setback was not Pulaski's lone difficulty. Shortages of everything drove him wild. When he commandeered horses (the best had been none too good for his men in Poland), he drew a rebuke from headquarters. Thoughtless of morale, he gathered around him gaudily dressed Europeans, inspiring hostility among his American officers. He made reports when it suited his whim. Believing himself subordinate to Washington alone, he scrapped haughtily with Anthony Wayne for daring to order him around during a mission.

The rift with Wayne mended quickly, though in a similar mood of wounded pride he wrote his sister: "I do not expect to stay here long. The customs here do not agree with my humor. Besides, there is a positive loss of time in this service. It is impossible to do anything good. The people here are too jealous. Everyone in the whole army is against me."

One of his officers, Benjamin Tallmadge, wrote a friend that "unless we change our present Commander, I fear we shall not be respectable."

After five months Pulaski resigned—with two conditions: first, that he retain his rank of brigadier general, and second, that he be permitted to raise an independent legion of sixty-eight cavalry armed with lances and two hundred light infantry. Washington agreed, believing Pulaski might still be "extremely useful."

Now Pulaski had the chance to prove that the methods of combat which had won him renown on the plains of Poland would work in America. He chose for officers mostly men who had served in European armies and who knew his mode of war. He recruited more soldiers than he had hoped for—three hundred and thirty. The problem of supply, his old nemesis, tormented him anew. He had no patience with paperwork, and Congress pestered him for receipts. Couldn't they *see* the things he had bought!

At last he received field orders. The legion advanced to Egg Harbor in New Jersey to oust four hundred Tories under nerveless Patrick Ferguson. On October 15, Pulaski's practice of recruiting British deserters (a policy frowned upon by Washington) boomeranged. One of his turncoats defected back to the enemy and persuaded Ferguson into a surprise attack. The legion was shattered in its first action.

Pulaski toyed with the idea of returning to Europe as he soulfully went about picking up the pieces. In November the world brightened again. Washington sent him to Minisink on the Delaware River to suppress Indian raids. He was completely on his own at last!

As the rebuilt legion pushed deep into the unending wilderness, reality once more cooled Pulaski's enthusiasm. His cavalry struggled forward in single file over rocks and stumps and clawing undergrowth. His runway to glory was nothing better than a jungly bypath that exhausted his patrols after three or four miles. Cole's Fort, his headquarters, turned out to be an astonishing edifice of stockades. After two weeks of waiting to fight an unseen foe, he wrote Congress for reassignment "near the enemy's lines," for here was "nothing but bears to fight."

Britain's move against the south retrieved Pulaski from loathsome inactivity. He fared badly in the successful defense of Charleston, and in October, 1779, he watched the assault against Savannah.

He had the remnants of his legion poised to throw into the battle when he learned French Admiral d'Estaing had fallen wounded. The French had lost their leader, the Americans were reeling back. Casimir Pulaski, alight with the sublime and tragic hope of somehow helping America, sought to yank victory out of chaos.

Leaving a colonel in charge of his men, he bravely galloped with an aide toward the French lines. A grapeshot struck him in the groin before he had covered twenty yards.

For the handsome Polish Count the long odyssey of disappointments, obstructions, and glory withheld came to an end. He died aboard the American ship *Wasp* and on the way to Charleston was buried at sea off the coast of Georgia.

ANTHONY WAYNE
Bayonets at Stony Point

THE BRITISH WERE TOO BUSY FORTIFYING STONY POINT
on the Hudson River to sense anything odd.

Dogs were part of every army camp, prowling near
kitchens, quick to snatch scraps and bones. Dogs were like
pieces of unused equipment, seen but not noticed—and not
missed for a long time.

When the dogs began to disappear from Stony Point, it
didn't occur to the Redcoats to wonder why. By July 14,
1779, nary a cur trotted about the garrison. Not a dog
lived within three miles.

American scouts had slain every one. A chance bark
might sound a warning, and General Anthony Wayne had
a deep, deep passion for surprise.

Wayne shared knowledge of the forthcoming assault on
Stony Point with his top officers only. The men knew
absolutely nothing. On the morning of the 15th, the
battalions were ordered out with full rations for inspection.

BORN: January 1, 1745, Waynesboro, Pa.
DIED: December 15, 1796, Presque Isle, Pa.

The inspection lasted until noon. When it was over, the 1,350 picked light infantrymen expected to return to their brush shelters to eat lunch. Instead they were faced south and marched.

Behind the column joggled two guns. They would not be used, for Wayne placed little faith in artillery. He believed the Continentals must rely on swiftness. In his philosophy of war, the will of the Redcoats to fight on must be broken by wearing-down tactics, by chipping the flanks and rear.

From his bivouac at Sandy Beach, Wayne marched on deer trails through a hilly wilderness. After five miles he allowed the only rest. By eight at night he reached the farm of David Springsteel. From there, in daylight, Stony Point could be seen below, a mile and a half away.

The previous month the British had seized the Point and the headland opposite in the first northern military operation after a winter and spring of inactivity. Crouched on the facing promontories, the British could choke off water transportation to West Point, the primary American stronghold in 1779.

Wayne's men now learned what was in store for them. The general who championed darting blows was preparing to launch the classic assault of the Revolution. Silence, darkness, and the naked bayonet were to be the weapons.

The orders were read. The first five men to breach Stony Point would receive $500, $400, $300, $200, and $100, in order of entry, and to the very first, a promotion besides.

Except for Major Hardy Murfree's battalion, which was to create a diversion, no soldier was to carry a loaded musket. Any man caught with ball and paper down his barrel was to be killed instantly. Any man who retreated one foot was to be put to death by the nearest officer.

Wayne meant it. A streak of purest killer ran in him. Before the war he had been the spoiled, headstrong heir to a Pennsylvania tannery. On the battlefield he had found his life's goal. Canada, Brandywine, and Valley Forge had enhanced his stature. He had stumbled in the fog at Germantown, and at Paoli . . .

At Paoli he had thoughtlessly stationed his men in front of their campfires to meet the enemy. Silhouetted thus, they made superb targets for the enemy under General Charles Grey. Grey had forbidden flints in order that no gun could be fired too soon. A quarter of Wayne's force fell to "No Flint" Grey's bayonets in a sickening slaughter.

One German had gleefully written how he stuck the rebels "like so many pigs, one after another, until the blood ran out of the touch-hole in my musket."

Paoli scarred Wayne's memory. He could threaten with death the soldier who carried a loaded musket. He was to order many soldiers shot down in cold blood during a mutiny of the Pennsylvania line the following year. Discipline in his book began with thirty-nine lashes. Yet he never forgot the horror worked by the Germans on his defeated soldiers.

Remember Paoli . . . ! Each man in the Stony Point assault force, remembering, soberly fastened a piece of paper to his hat to distinguish him from the enemy. At exactly eleven thirty P. M. Wayne took a position in front of the leading column. He gave the command, "Forward!"

The columns marched silently, the men with sharpened bayonets, the officers with short-handled spears and swords. Directly behind Wayne came men carrying poles tipped with hooks for clearing away the enemy's barricade of logs and brush.

The hot night air lay heavy and starless. It seemed as black as the last hour of earth to the anxious men. They kept their feet going, holding their muskets tightly and struggling to forget the odds against surviving a hand-to-hand fight.

A mile from Stony Point the force split into three groups. Ahead of each group moved one hundred men to clear the

obstructions. Ahead of the one hundred probed a spear-
head of twenty men and an officer with the job of killing
sentries.

Soon the soldiers began to make out the inky, sinister
shapes of the fortifications. Some eight batteries had been
erected on the summit. A line of abatis curved from one
side to the other, and a similar line protected three small
works farther down the slope. The whole was on an island
of one hundred acres, three quarters surrounded by the
Hudson River. On the inland side, a swamp separated it
from the New Jersey shore.

High tide had submerged the sand bars by which Wayne
had expected to cross the two hundred yards of swamp.
Silently the men waded in, sinking to the waist. They
stumbled against thick marsh grasses that whipped their
thighs and roused tiny splashes.

The columns sloshed on. Wet night clasped at farm boys
accustomed to sundrops and rabbits running. Now each
stride pulled closer the ghastly, unreal climax of killing
and dying.

A splash . . . too loud. British sentries called out. Guns
opened fire on the hillside. Flares shot up. Suddenly the
nightmare of suspense was shattered by firing, shouting, and
splashing.

Murfree's "forlorn hopes" dashed at the bridge on the
causeway, creating a diversion at the western tip. The
British were fooled into thinking that Murfree led the main
assault.

Still, Wayne's column absorbed murderous fire. Seventeen of the twenty-man advance squad fell. Artillery roared
above the rattle of musketry. Wayne's men charged from
the water and gained the trees. Closer, boys, closer . . . the
bayonet is short.

Wayne was hit in the face and toppled. "March on!" he
ordered. "Carry me to the fort!"

Bayonets glinted in the flashes of artillery. Bayonets

clanked against cannon, shifted and stuck. Strong-wristed farm boys pitchforked the gunners like straw dummies.

The main body of defenders doubled back. Too late. The Americans poured in. *"Remember Paoli!"*

The confused British heard the cry and remembered, too. Lieutenant Colonel Henry Johnson, his face white as he stared at the spear poked against his breast, surrendered the fort and his 543 survivors. The cringing Redcoats hurled down their muskets. "Mercy, dear Americans!"

The bleeding Wayne shouted an order. It stayed the bayonets. Stony Point was his.

In a week patriotic lips throughout the North were warbling the catch line, "All hearts burn to emulate our Wayne."

The same lips were presently calling him "Mad Anthony," a nickname hung upon him by a drunken Irish scout called Jemmey Rover. "Is Anthony mad?" demanded Jemmey after Wayne had jailed him for the blind staggers. Wayne was not insane, but he had an explosive temper. Men ducked when he encountered disobedience or cowardice, for he scattered his wrath like shrapnel.

Mad Anthony became Commander in Chief of the United States Army in 1792. He subdued the northwest Indians in 1795. Yet none of his later triumphs compare with the fantastic bayonet assault upon Stony Point.

He did not let the memory of the Paoli slaughter twist him when he had the British helpless. He refused to act the butcher despite a wound that must have cried for instant vengeance. When mercy was asked, American bayonets rested.

By his conduct at Stony Point, Anthony Wayne helped fix the national character. He taught the British and he taught the world that bravery and patriotism are not the only American virtues. Humanity is too.

WALTER BUTLER

Tory Ranger

FOR GENERATIONS AFTER THE REVOLUTION, WALTER
Butler trod the backcountry of New York and Pennsylvania
with the blood of unnumbered innocents squishing in his
shoes.

Sinister legends collected about the memory of this
American-born fighter for the King. Forty years after his
death Timothy Dwight, president of Yale, vengefully
concocted a tale of Butler's slaying. Dwight's account,
inaccurate in both time and place, has Butler abjectly
pleading for his life.

In Butler's own day, General William Heath thought
that he "seems to have been the most ruthless" of the
loyalist leaders. Heath carefully selected the word "seems."
Facts about the supposed monster were always hard
come by.

The date of Butler's birth is not recorded. The location
of his grave, if grave he had, is unknown. No artist painted

BORN: 1752 (?)
DIED: October 30, 1781, West Canada Creek, N.Y.

his portrait. No writer described the color of his hair or the breadth of his shoulders or jotted down a favorite mannerism.

He is the midnight marauder, part phantom and part devil, sneaking light as a panther through the hemlocks with his Rangers and Indians. When he lay a mutilated corpse by West Canada Creek, did some slender maiden sob through the long nights?

Barely a dozen of his letters survive. He kept only one campaign journal. Once, long after the Wyoming Massacre in Pennsylvania in July, 1778, he was goaded to a rare defense when the outcry over his cruelty continued to grow. He denied any atrocity. Still, he made it perfectly clear that if anyone calls "inhumanity the killing of men in arms in the field, we in that case plead guilty."

His defense of Wyoming is abbreviated. It ignores his Indian allies. They launched war canoes into the Susquehanna, paddled down fleeing "men in arms," and reaped 227 scalps.

Walter Butler excelled in combat. He is a killer rather than a soldier primarily because he killed in the wrong cause—for King George III; and he killed in the wrong war—the ceaseless, murky civil war of neighbor against neighbor. Both the Continentals and the British professionals won honors for feats of valor. Even the behind-the-scenes sorties of the patriots emerge as heroic deeds despite diabolical savagery because their side won. In war, might makes right.

Walter Butler fought fire with fire. His name embodied all the horrors of the frontier struggle because his side lost and not because his principle was misguided. Tragically for him (and other loyalists) the legend makers were not his comrades but his enemies.

At the outset of the Revolution, Walter Butler was a budding lawyer in Albany. His father, John Butler, was next to the Johnsons the most powerful man in the Mohawk Valley of New York. The Butlers, father and son, declared for the King. Along with other loyalist leaders, they fled to Canada. Operating usually from a base at Fort Niagara, they uncoiled the swift, ravaging blows known as the "War out of Niagara."

New York, the last state to assent to the Declaration of Independence, was a loyalist stronghold. (It contributed 23,500 troops to the British and 17,700 to the Continental armies.) To secure the state, rebel Committees of Safety ferreted out the disloyal. Butler's mother and sister were among those removed to Albany and imprisoned as hostages for the safety of the frontiers.

Many loyalist wives and children, unable to endure the strenuous migration to Canada, remained in the Mohawk Valley. Their undefended homesteads offered rich opportunities to lawless men for murder and plunder. The worst curse was the Indians.

The Six Nations stretched their lands across northwestern New York. They spilled two thousand warriors into the maimed Valley. Britain, with its ready-made system of Indian Superintendencies, engaged the allegiance of the Indians at the start, but never held better than the loosest control. The Americans foolishly hoped to keep the Indians neutral. Soon the absurdity of such a policy was fatally evident. By 1777 the active aid of about three hundred Oneidas was obtained.

As a boy Walter Butler had frequently accompanied his father in the conduct of Indian affairs for the King. He had early learned the wisdom of having the savages on his side. Before many Revolutionary frays, however, he swore never to embark upon an expedition in which the Indians held the majority.

Disciplining the redskins was nigh impossible. They never mastered their fear of artillery, and except in special situations were next to worthless. Hordes of war parties, ranging from fifty to two hundred braves, made independent attacks upon the Valley constantly.

The atrocities inflicted by the Indians seem to have stemmed from their desire to avenge Oriskany. There, on August 6, 1777, St. Leger's campaign to reach a junction with Burgoyne at Albany received a fiery jolt. In the battle his Senecas suffered terrible slaughter. Ensign Walter Butler of the King's (or 8th) Regiment escaped unscathed and promptly volunteered for a bold mission.

At the head of about fifteen braves and whites, he started down the Mohawk River to the settlement at German Flats. He intended to live off the country, meanwhile recruiting a Tory force under the nose of the enemy. On a torrid night he held a meeting at the home of Rudolph Shoemaker, once a King's justice of the peace. While he explained the need for men, the perspiring loyalists cast fearful glances now and again at Butler's painted Senecas. Had they instead looked outside, they might have spied rebel soldiers under Colonel James Weston surrounding the house.

Taken prisoner, Butler was court-martialed and sentenced to be hanged as a spy. Friends of his Albany law days interceded, and he was imprisoned in the town. When he grew sick, the friends contrived his transfer to a private home. His host nursed loyalist sympathies, apparently. For one night in late April, Walter Butler stepped past a drunken sentry. He had a pocketful of money and a dagger in his belt. He mounted a horse and rode through melting snow to a reunion with his father in Quebec.

The year of his escape, 1778, was also the year he sowed the seeds of the evil that is his memorial. He participated in the Wyoming Massacre on July 3. And on November 11, a day of sleet and rain, he soaked Cherry Valley in blood.

Located near Otsego Lake, Cherry Valley had importance as a link in the short chain of outposts guarding Albany. Its fort consisted of a newly built stockade encircling the village meetinghouse.

Walter Butler, now a captain, marched one hundred and fifty miles from a starting point by the Chemung River. He had his first command—some three hundred of his father's Tory Rangers. Near what is now Windsor, New York, he made contact with Joseph Brant, the blood-curdling Mohawk Chief. Butler amazingly talked Brant into a subordinate role, though the chief led nearly five hundred Indians and was his senior in rank.

Violating his rule never to let Indians dominate, Butler opened the attack on Cherry Valley before noon. He failed to subdue the fort for want of artillery and the main effort shifted to the village. All forty dwellings, along with every other building and barn, were sacked and burned. Livestock was rounded up and driven off. For weeks afterward, bodies were still being discovered in the woods.

It is doubtful if any women and children were deliberately harmed, though terrified they all must have been. In the retreat over the frozen trails to Niagara, Butler took along two women and their seven children. Perhaps he thought to exchange them for the hostages held in Albany—his mother and the wives of many of his Rangers.

Not until his last action was Butler again in the Mohawk Valley. Yet many of the horrors committed there during these next thirty-six months were attributed to him.

A fighter, not a saint, Butler volunteered for duty at Albany, Fort Pitt, and Detroit. He eagerly served in the upper posts, which less dedicated loyalists as eagerly tried to dodge.

He died at twenty-eight, successfully covering the retreat of Major John Ross during a raid into the Valley. He gave his life for a principle—and for a country he longed to see but never did.

A Continental soldier shot him while he was defending a ford at West Canada Creek. His scalp was borne in triumph to Albany a hundred miles away.

He had been denounced by the enemy for using Indians. What may be said of the Oneida ally of the Continental Army who carved off the top of his head?

In an article announcing his death at West Canada Creek, the New York *Packet* for November 8, 1781, states the case for allies in all wars. And, tacitly, for all enemies.

"The Oneida Indians behaved well in the action and deserve much credit."

JOHN PAUL JONES
Indomitable Sailor

AT THREE P.M. ENEMY SHIPS WERE SIGHTED OFF THE EAST
coast of England. An hour later officers and men of the
American flagship *Bonhomme Richard* took battle stations.
Marine drummers paraded up and down the frigate beat-
ing the roll to General Quarters.

The sun lowered into the North Sea. Commodore John
Paul Jones, foremost sea captain of the meager Continental
Navy, terror of British commerce, and idol of the ladies of
Paris, raised the signal flags: FORM LINE OF BATTLE.

The signal was roundly ignored. The captains of his
squadron, composed of two small frigates, *Alliance* and
La Pallas, and a corvette, *Vengeance*, did exactly as they
thought prudent. Willful misunderstanding and outright
disobedience were not rare in the navies of the day. Should
a battle lie at hand, John Paul Jones was going to have to
start it himself.

Jones took his post on the quarterdeck, where he looked

BORN: July 6, 1747, Arbigland, Scotland
DIED: July 18, 1792, Paris, France

like a mistake. But his short, spare frame was knit without a fiber of flinch. He was the best fighter of single ship-to-ship engagements of his era, and he crowded every sail in the effort to close.

Ten miles away glittered forty-one prizes. Five weeks earlier, on August 14, 1779, Jones had begun this bold raid up the west coast of Ireland and around Scotland. He had bagged seventeen British merchantmen. Those feats and all he had done on his other cruises resembled lean pickings compared to the forty-one sails now standing in his direction.

From two captured British pilots he had learned about the ships ahead. They were a convoy from the Baltic with supplies for the British navy. To get within hurting range, Jones knew he must deal with the two escorts, the powerful frigate *Serapis* and the sloop of war *Countess of Scarborough*.

Captain Richard Pearson of *Serapis* ordered his convoy to hug the shore. He signaled *Countess of Scarborough* to join him and cleared to action.

Although outnumbered in warships four to two, Pearson, shrewd as he was gallant, had noted the temperamental conduct of *La Pallas*, *Alliance*, and *Vengeance*. He pointed *Serapis* for *Bonhomme Richard*.

From bow to stern, *Serapis* enjoyed vast superiority. *Bonhomme Richard*, a worn-out East Indiaman, had been rearmed by Jones and renamed in honor of Ben Franklin's pen name (Poor Richard). *Serapis* was newer and larger. She mounted more and bigger guns. And owing to her slippery copper-sheathed bottom, a recent invention of the British, she was swifter and more maneuverable.

Jones estimated that his best chance was to board and grapple. With guns shotted and ready, *Bonhomme Richard* sailed slowly before a light breeze, grandly gliding with the dying sun through the last hours of her life.

By six thirty P.M. the two ships were side by side, a pistol shot apart. "What ship is that?" hailed Captain Pearson.

Jones had one of his officers reply, "*The Princess Royal!*" He had a fine sense of deception. *Bonhomme Richard* flew British colors. Her officers wore the blue-and-white uniforms of 1777, which resembled those of the British.

"Where from?" bellowed Pearson. When no answer came, he shouted again, "Answer immediately, or I shall be under the necessity of firing into you."

Jones struck the British colors and had the red-white-and-blue striped American ensign hoisted. He ordered a starboard broadside. *Serapis* fired almost the same instant.

In the opening salvos, Jones suffered a misfortune that increased the odds against him. A pair of his 18-pounders burst. Several gunners died, the battery was wrecked, and part of the deck blown off.

For nearly an hour each captain sought to rake by swinging across the other's bow or stern. Neither succeeded completely. The passes convinced Jones of the impossibility of outmaneuvering the nimble *Serapis*, or of surviving a gun duel.

He tried to board, but was repulsed. After a period of firing and maneuvering, Pearson cried, "Have you struck?"

John Paul Jones filled his lungs and retorted, "I have not yet begun to fight!"

Jones pivoted on *Serapis'* bowsprit, still trying to rake and come alongside. The ships collided, bow to stern. The starboard anchor of the Englishman caught in the bulwarks of the American's starboard quarter.

By this quirk of fortune, the ships were locked in a lethal embrace, their topsides brushing. The muzzles of their guns bumped. The lone chance for Jones to win, by boarding and grappling, was his.

It was now past eight P.M. The opening guns had attracted throngs to Flamborough Head, a wide headland of chalk cliffs four hundred and fifty feet high. A harvest moon had risen over a cloudy eastern horizon, and from the cliffs the spectators had a fine view of the naval battle mottling the glassy smooth sea with sudden orange blotches and drifts of gunpowder.

While *Bonhomme Richard* and *Serapis* wrestled, the American ships acted independently. The corvette *Vengeance* withdrew to a safe distance. *La Pallas* engaged *Countess of Scarborough*. *Alliance*, under Captain Pierre Landais, a man of diseased mind, turned on her flagship.

Three times Landais darted in and fired broadsides, holing *Bonhomme Richard* below the waterline and killing many sailors. Later the madman confided that he hoped to sink Jones, capture the crippled *Serapis* himself, and take all the credit.

Landais' attack left *Bonhomme Richard* mortally leaking. Her master-at-arms released the prize ship prisoners, numbering one hundred, and hurried them to the pumps. One escaped in the melee and informed Captain Pearson that *Bonhomme Richard* had five feet of water in her hold. A few minutes more and Jones must strike or sink.

Jones's plight was every bit as critical as the prisoner reported. Below, his hold was flooded; above, fires edged his sails. The decks swam with blood. Fragments of rigging and spars crashed continually from the sky.

The heaviest guns of the *Serapis*, her 18-pounders, riddled Jones's topsides. He was powerless to stop the destruction. For fire power he had to rely upon the marksmanship of the French marine musketeers on deck and the seamen in the tops. All his cannon were silenced except three 9-pounders on the quarterdeck. Jones handled one himself, aiming double-headed shot against the mainmast of *Serapis*.

Any other captain would have quit. Prisoners ran loose, officers in powder-blackened uniforms reeled in shock, chiefs cried for quarter. But John Paul Jones got the most out of any ship, and he still had a ship under him, even if only a few stanchions kept the quarterdeck from collapsing into the gun room and the main deck from sagging into the hold.

Jones determined to conquer or sink. Born in Scotland, the son of a gardener, he knew that to strike meant sacrificing his hard-earned reputation as a naval officer. Like so many other men without high-placed friends, he had followed the sea only to improve his lot in life.

Performing on the quarterdeck of *Bonhomme Richard*, he was a white light amid the burning tints of red and orange. He inspired all in his crew. On other days he had maddened them by his refusal to reward good work with so much as a pat on the back, by his red-flag temper, by his threats to shoot sailors whom he believed ignorant or disobedient, by his demands for perfection.

During the moonlit night of September 23, 1779, Commodore Jones, handling the 9-pounder while his ship shuddered and creaked and crashed about him, was as near to the perfect fighting sailor as the centuries have witnessed.

Captain Pearson could not match him. No man could. At ten thirty P.M. Pearson's nerve broke. He struck, though he still had four 18-pounders blazing, and half the men of the *Bonhomme Richard* lay dead or wounded.

The Baltic convoy had slipped through without loss during battle. But the other British warship, *Countess of Scarborough*, surrendered to *La Pallas*. Jones transferred to *Serapis*, and thirty-six hours later *Bonhomme Richard* went under the North Sea.

John Paul Jones was never to participate in another major naval action during the Revolution. A free-lance adventurer, he served afterward in the Russian navy and died in Paris. It is as an American naval hero, though, that his fame endures.

By refusing to quit off Flamborough Head, he won the epic battle of the age of sail.

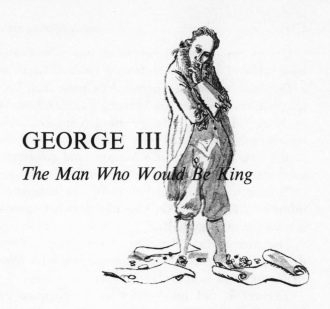

GEORGE III
The Man Who Would Be King

"THE CLEVEREST TUTORS IN THE WORLD COULD HAVE DONE little, probably, to expand that small intellect."

So reflected novelist William Makepeace Thackeray on the backward youngster who would become George III, America's last king.

George early exhibited the slow mind which, being unequal to the demands of the crown, would finally take refuge in madness. He could not read until eleven, but he mastered subjects that did not contain motion or theory. He loved geography and drawing maps. He memorized his family history, though without suspecting its evil taints.

His dynasty, the House of Hanover, was barely royal and hardly ever noble. His great-grandfather, George I, had by a wisp of ancestry swung from the Electorship of Hanover to the English throne, and he dutifully avoided governing. His grandfather, George II, counted his treasury coin by coin. His father, a patron of fortunetellers and bull-baiting, died while Prince of Wales.

BORN: June 4, 1738, London, England
DIED: January 29, 1820, London, England

Little George was the first of his line to be born in England. This "English drone from a German hive" inherited a Teutonic concern for detail. As George III, his clerkish mind quivered under his Mamma's exhortation, "George, be King!" He tried. He did his groping best. He industriously mixed facts and lofty intentions as if by dieting on such a stew he could please Mamma and grow into the all-knowing monarch, a true patriot king.

"I wish to do nothing but good," he assured his prime minister. "Therefore everyone who does not agree with me is a traitor or a scoundrel."

The Americans, therefore, were both. "Blows must decide," he asserted. "Once these rebels have felt a smart blow, they will submit."

The rebels did not submit under England's opening blows. On the contrary, they issued a declaration of independence and termed George "A Prince . . . unfit to be the ruler of a free people."

Month after month the English public waited for news of a great victory. Instead the dispatches from America ran over with lists of wounded and killed. France entered the war on the side of the rebels.

The King blinked his bulging gray eyes and stared at his favorite map. If America succeeded in casting off her dependence, then the West Indies and Ireland would soon follow. "This island would be reduced to itself," he mused, "and soon would be a poor island indeed."

Parliament pitched with talk of peace. George's mood slipped from haughty determination to edgy defensiveness. "I will never consent that in any treaty that may be concluded a single word be mentioned concerning Canada, Nova Scotia, or Florida," he declared. By these outposts, George expected to "keep a certain awe over the abandoned colonies."

As a warrior-king, he did what he could. He noted all

the periods and commas—the purchases of recruits and supplies, the dates of sailings, the news of privateers.

Alas, he could not penetrate to the heart of the trouble: his generals were mediocre. They were nearly as weak as his ministers and himself. Unlike Abraham Lincoln ninety years later, George could not find a strongman, an enemy killer in the mold of U. S. Grant.

Gage, Burgoyne, and Howe sailed home with reputations blasted. Clinton sat entrenched in New York and wondered what Washington was up to. Rhode Island's Greene maneuvered through the south. The most aggressive of the Redcoats were those stumbling about Virginia under Cornwallis.

The war puttered on. George III found his inability to win lying like a canker upon his concept of a king. A king must be omnipotent! Blankly he proclaimed that "this long contest will end as it ought, by the colonists returning to the mother country."

Cornwallis surrendered at Yorktown. Lord North moaned, "Oh, God, it is all over." George innocently thought the war could be pursued from bases in New York and Charleston.

Parliament heard him and decided otherwise. On December 5, 1782, he sat on his throne and huskily proclaimed that the independence of America would be recognized.

The conviction that he had discharged his duty as king saved his sanity. He adjusted to the separation of the colonies without ever becoming reconciled to it.

By 1783 a third of George's sixty-year reign had passed. He had lost the vast American colonies, and his popularity had drained almost to the bottom. Even his liberal use of bribes, or "gold pills," could no longer cure his troubles in Parliament and simply dragged him deeper into debt. John Wilkes and Edmund Burke plagued him. The

mysterious letter writer, "Junius," had disappeared from
the pages of the *Public Advertiser*, but a cruder and more
relentless attack flowed from the satirical pen of cartoonist
James Gillray.

Twice the hapless George considered abdicating. Luckily
he now made his one brilliant appointment. Overcoming
his animosity for Lord Chatham, he named Chatham's son,
William Pitt the Younger, prime minister. Relieved of the
business of state by the phenomenal young man of twenty-
four, the King's popularity rose.

His private life appealed to a nation of farmers and
shopkeepers. He regularly attended church. He enjoyed
hunting and fishing, and he could dance to the same tune
for three hours. His domestic life was calm. In faithfulness
to his troth he set a standard new to the courts of England.

His marriage to the homely Charlotte Sophia of Meck-
lenburg-Strelitz had worked out well, though she had not
been his first choice. In 1761 he had fallen timidly in love
with the flashing but nonroyal Lady Sarah Lennox. After
his proposal had been accepted, Mamma said no, Lady
Sue would not do as queen. The son had consoled his true
love with a post as bridesmaid.

The skinny little Queen Charlotte and the tall, shambling
King George were devoted parents to an odd and wicked
brood. The outspoken Duke of Wellington called the
King's sons "the damnedest millstones about the neck of
any government that can be imagined."

George bore stoically with his sorry pack of offspring,
demanding only that they should not want courage.
Bravery was the part of the kingly pose he could handle.
On six occasions when assassins sought his life, he demonstrated amazing self-control.

A barber's daughter, deluded into the idea that the
throne was rightfully hers, stabbed at him with a knife in
1786. "The poor creature is mad! Do not hurt her. She has

not hurt me," he shouted to the enraged mob that seized her. Four years later he was stoned. In 1795 he was again stoned and fired upon while in the royal coach. He coolly picked a stone from his lap and handed it to a fellow passenger with the words, "My lord, keep it as a memorandum of the civilities which we have received." In 1800 a crazed former soldier fired a pistol from the pit of Drury Lane Theater as the King entered his box. George shied back, then stepped forward to show himself unharmed. When the curtain rose, he promptly fell asleep, awakening at the end of the performance to "God Save the King."

With young Pitt guiding the ship of state, George's sense of inferiority increased. He had failed to live up to his childish, impossible ideal of a king—a superbeing of infallible decisions. He trod on marble and dressed in silks and stared at his subjects, and all the time he quietly wallowed in guilt.

One spring day in 1788 he stepped from his carriage in Windsor Park and sauntered to an oak tree. He chatted with the oak as if it were his cousin, Frederick the Great of Prussia. He was put in a straitjacket.

He had first tussled with madness back in 1765, shortly after his marriage. Altogether, he was to suffer five attacks, each of longer duration than the one previous. After 1788, the country supported him with affectionate pity.

In 1811 he went irrevocably insane. The Prince of Wales, "the most accomplished blackguard in Europe," governed as regent and impatiently waited for death to pass him the crown.

But the old King clung to life—or a kind of life—for a decade. A pathetic figure in a purple dressing gown and cap, his white beard nearly to his waist, he roved a wing of the palace, freed of his guilt at last.

The Queen visited him regularly, fussing and straightening. He took no notice of her. He thumped a harpsichord, piped on a flute, sang hymns, spoke with friends long dead. Mad, blind, deaf, he did not know when his wife died.

He did not know when America warred again with England. From 1811 until his death in 1820, the slow-witted man who had tried so hard to be King of England reigned supreme in a strange kingdom of his own.

BENEDICT ARNOLD

Glory Was Not Enough

THE OFFER SHOCKED BENEDICT ARNOLD. ASIDE FROM lowering his head, however, he betrayed no emotion.

Washington was mildly surprised at the mysterious reaction. Since he had no time to seek out the reason, he suggested Arnold await him at headquarters. They could talk over the matter there.

Arnold nodded. He watched, narrow-eyed, as Washington spurred off to observe the last detachment of Americans cross the Hudson River for the attack on New York.

The offer that Washington had just tendered was "a post of honor"—command of the left wing of the Continental Army. Arnold would have three divisions and the chance for glory beyond anything he had yet achieved. After startling feats of arms on remote battlefields, he would fight with the main army. Washington would see him in action.

But the Benedict Arnold of July 31, 1780, no longer

BORN: January 14, 1741, Norwich, Conn.
DIED: June 14, 1801, London, England

wanted to be under the eye of the Commander in Chief. What he had expected Washington to offer him was command of West Point.

All this he repeated to Washington's aides, and later that day to Washington. The Virginian listened, puzzled and curious but suspecting nothing, to the whining complaints of his talented problem child. He would, he said, reconsider the assignment.

The next day news of an enemy shift reached the American camp. The British had abandoned their expedition to Rhode Island as too risky and were returning to New York. In consequence, Washington suspended his plan to storm the city. His general orders for August 3, 1780, bore the sentence: "Major-General Arnold will take command of the garrison at West Point."

With such a tonic, Arnold's recovery was swift. West Point, "the key to the continent," was a salable piece of property, unlike three divisions, and Benedict Arnold intended to sell the fortress to the British.

At the heart of his unholy motives was a passion for honors quickly won. In early battles this passion had galvanized him into the best on-the-spot combat leader in the army. He could stand alone, as when he talked Ethan Allen and his rowdy Green Mountain Boys into sharing the capture of Fort Ticonderoga with him. He could cooperate, as with Richard Montgomery on the futile assault at Quebec. Adjusting to naval warfare with superb ease, he had constructed a flotilla on Lake Champlain and severely damaged a larger British fleet in the first naval action between England and America. His conduct, once the shooting started—especially at Saratoga—had transcended valor and soared into the realm of frenzy.

He could show his troops every kindness, though he drove them to the limit of endurance, if need be, as on the agonizing march to Quebec. Hungering for approval, he flared up at anyone who crossed him, superior officers or politicians. When Congress passed over him for promotion, he shook with mortification. When the Council of Pennsylvania accused him of misusing his rank and his men for personal gain, he demanded a court-martial to refute the charge.

The court-martial found him guilty of several offenses. Acting on the recommendation of Congress, Washington reprimanded Arnold, but with typical restraint. Nonetheless, to Arnold's hatred of politicians was now added the hatred of George Washington.

Even as he had been proclaiming his innocence, Arnold had entered into secret negotiations with British Commander in Chief Henry Clinton in May, 1779. To show good faith, he had regularly sent Clinton coded messages concerning American troops.

Arnold's price for a masterstroke was high. He had three children by his deceased first wife to support. He loved good living, and his second wife, the highborn Tory Peggy Shippen, who partnered his get-rich-quick schemes, liked expensive living.

Within a month after taking over West Point, Arnold learned that Clinton had agreed to his price. For West Point intact with a garrison of three thousand troops and all stores, the sum of twenty thousand pounds (ten thousand cash, ten thousand in defrayal of debts). Even if the plot failed, he was to receive half that sum.

Never one to pass up small change, Arnold sold, for cash, the pork, wine, and rum issued him from the West Point commissary. He sent to Philadelphia for Peggy to ease his anxiety while he hunted reliable go-betweens.

As he dickered with the British, a golden opportunity dropped into his lap. The Commander in Chief was to be at nearby Peekskill on September 17 on his way to meet the French leaders at Hartford. Washington desired a guard, and wrote, "You will keep this to yourself as I want to make my journey in secret."

Arnold straightaway dispatched the intelligence to the British. The momentous capture, however, was never ventured. Four days later Arnold met with British Major John André to arrange the final details of the West Point sellout.

The rendezvous was held the night of September 21 six miles below Stony Point. While the pair conferred in a copse of firs, a mishap occurred. *Vulture*, the British warship that had transported André, was chased several miles downriver by American light artillery. André was stranded amid the enemy.

Arnold scribbled two passes for him under the name "John Anderson" and hurried back to his headquarters. André, who wore civilian clothes, put the passes in his pocket and six documents from Arnold in his stockings. Then he started on the perilous overland route to his own lines.

On Monday morning, September 25, the bubble burst. Two young Continental officers interrupted Arnold's breakfast. They informed him that Washington would follow within half an hour. Arnold invited them to join him at the table. Almost immediately afterward a third officer entered the room.

He handed some letters to Arnold. The traitor opened one. A "John Anderson" had been captured carrying a pass signed by Arnold and papers containing vital information about West Point. The papers had been sent to Washington.

His swarthy face oddly blank, Arnold mumbled an excuse. He hobbled upstairs and acquainted Peggy with the disaster. Telling the young officers that he would return shortly, he galloped for the river, leaped aboard his barge, and was rowed to the British sloop of war *Vulture* off Tellers Point.

The treachery of a leading major general stunned the people. They united, at first, in violence. Arnold was hanged in effigy in countless cities. A mob broke into the cemetery at Norwich and threw away the gravestones of Arnold's father and infant brother (who died before the traitor's birth) because both were named Benedict Arnold. Marksmen practiced on targets shaped like Arnold's head.

In time the violence boiled off, leaving a toughened unity among Americans. Arnold's act wiped out political tolerance. Henceforth a Tory was an enemy.

Arnold felt no remorse. What he had tried to do was right for him and therefore right for the nation. He was a standard unto himself and could do no wrong. If he felt anything, it was remorse at being denied the full price of success.

The British commissioned him brigadier general of provincial troops. He went on a marauding expedition into Virginia and burned Richmond; he led a diversionary attack against Connecticut and burned New London. Knowing what his fate would be if captured did not impair either his skill or his courage.

Arnold asked a rebel prisoner what his (Arnold's) fate would be if the Americans captured him. "They would cut off that leg (wounded at Quebec and Saratoga) and bury it with honor," answered the prisoner. "Then they would hang the rest of you on a gibbet."

In December, 1781, Arnold sailed with his family for England. He gave expert counsel on the continuance of the war till the government favorable to him lost power. Under the new party he was rejected and scorned.

His post-Revolutionary career encountered obstacle after obstacle. Despite an ambition that never broke stride, his mercantile enterprises lagged.

He continued to flare up at slights. In 1792, he defied death on an English dueling ground. Having shot and missed, he stood defenseless and demanded an apology so forcefully that his awed opponent laid aside his unfired pistol and expressed regret that there had been a misunderstanding.

Tossed by frustration and unhappiness, Benedict Arnold died in London in 1801. Had he fallen at Saratoga in 1777, he would have left on the roll of Revolutionary immortals a name second only to George Washington.

He left instead the synonym for treason.

HAYM SALOMON

Servant of Liberty

IN THE POCKETS OF CONGRESSMAN JAMES MADISON WERE a handkerchief, a bunch of papers, and some keys. He had not a cent to pay for his lodgings as he dragged his feet along the cobblestones of Philadelphia. The man who would become fourth President of the United States hated to borrow money. His pride burned at having to seek it from a stranger . . .

Along Front Street between Market and Arch he hesitated at an open door, the office of Haym Salomon, commission agent, dealer in securities, ship broker, and son of liberty. Madison braced himself and entered.

How much money did he want? asked Salomon, a small brown-eyed man with a harsh cough. When Madison told him, Salomon put the amount into his hand.

Madison inquired about the terms. Salomon replied there were none. The money could be repaid anytime, without interest. The current rates of interest, said Salomon,

BORN: ca. 1740, Lissa, Poland
DIED: January 6, 1785, Philadelphia, Pa.

were too high and he ignored them. Besides, he was happy
to be able to help anyone serving the country.

Madison protested, but to no avail. Uncomfortable and
vaguely irked, he departed with his money.

An hour later a messenger arrived at Salomon's office.
Robert Morris, Superintendent of the Treasury, must see
him at once. Salomon pulled on his coat and hastened, as
he had so many times, to Morris' office.

Morris had a bill of exchange, which he wanted Salomon
to sell for the government. Like Madison, Morris had used
Salomon only as a last resort. Other brokers were impossible
with their charge of one and a half to two percent commission. Salomon charged the government a quarter
percent, if anything, despite the ever-present risk of
personal ruin.

Congress had first tried to finance the war by printing
press, running off bushels of paper money. Having no real
backing, the Continental paper money fell in value.
Counterfeiters, both British and American, quickened the
decline. (Counterfeit bills were distinguished by better
paper and superior engraving!) By 1781, Continental paper
money was worth about five cents a pound. Barbers bought
it for shaving paper.

The bill of exchange, which Salomon handled so out-
standingly, came to be relied upon more and more. It got
money into the Treasury quickly. It was like an I.O.U.
That is, it was a piece of paper that bore the promise to
pay the bearer the face amount. If France, for example,
loaned America five thousand dollars, it did not send cash
across the ocean. It sent a bill of exchange for five thousand
dollars. To convert the bill of exchange into hard cash
(foreign money, gold, or silver), the government had to
sell it to the highest bidder. The new owner paid in hard
cash and then either claimed the sum from France or resold
it at a profit.

Along with international loans, the bill of exchange was used in private business. A French merchant, or one in the West Indies, might make payment in a bill of exchange. Whether an international loan or a business transaction, the seller had to endorse the bill. He had to make himself responsible for payment if the foreign nation or merchant refused to pay.

Haym Salomon was the most successful broker in Philadelphia. Time and again he saved the day for Morris with his swift check. He knew how to sell the bills of exchange to best advantage for the government. He never sold too cheaply, for tomorrow there would be other bills to sell, and the market must be kept high. He sold bills when no one else could, when confidence in the cause of independence fell before British land and sea victories.

And when he could not sell a bill, he advanced the money himself. A total of $211,678.00 went from his pocket into the Treasury.

Day by day, Morris came to depend on Salomon more and more. "I sent for Haym Salomon" was like a refrain in Morris' diary. Sometimes the men conferred five and six times a day. If Morris had an important message to send to New York, he sent it by Salomon. If he had a new crisis in the Treasury to tide over, he sent for Salomon.

Once in desperation he sent for Salomon on Yom Kippur, highest of holy days in the Jewish religion. The messenger knocked on the door of the synagogue (a rented room in Sterling Alley) while the congregation was at worship.

To do business on Yom Kippur was outrageous. Everyone was shocked at Morris, including Salomon. But the need of the government for funds was urgent. Slowly he walked to the front of the worshipers.

He spoke of the Jews in other countries. They built homes, prospered, aided good causes, harmed nobody.

And then, under the excuse of a difference in religion, they were beaten, exiled, tortured, or murdered for their possessions.

Here was a new country, a new start for all groups, Salomon reminded the congregation. The Jews numbered only a small segment of the population—barely 2,500 in 3,000,000. Yet the Jews were serving in the Continental Army in greater numbers, proportionately, than any other group. In America, the Jews could belong.

The next day Haym Salomon brought to Robert Morris the money he requested—money raised on the floor of the synagogue on the most sacred Jewish day of the year!

To perform his wizardry for Robert Morris, Salomon had to maintain his personal credit at the bank, his standing as a businessman. So he betook himself regularly to the coffeehouse near his office. Brokers and merchants gathered in the coffeehouses of Philadelphia to exchange news about markets, to buy and sell, to hear the best opinions of world finance.

When he had first arrived penniless in America three years before the war, he had sat in the coffeehouses and listened. The other brokers had elaborately ignored the expressionless little man. He continued to come there, his keen eyes and ears missing nothing, his mind sifting and weighing and deciding.

He spoke several tongues, but the languages he understood best were the delicate idioms of international commerce and banking. He adjusted instinctively to the fluctuations of many currencies. He grasped supply and demand—what fetched a better price in the West Indies than in Portugal, in Cuba than in Spain.

His corner in the Front Street coffeehouse altered gradually from a spot to be avoided to a spot men sought out.

They knew his ability. They did not know what he thought of them as they fattened their purses on war profits and ardently espoused a single cause, themselves.

The little man sitting with his pot of coffee understood about freedom. As a youth he had fought for liberty in his native Poland. When his country fell under Russian control, he fled to England and thence to America.

Four years later, on September 22, 1776, he was arrested by the British as a rebel spy. Paroled, he was jailed again in August, 1778, and condemned to death for plotting to burn British warships and warehouses in Philadelphia. He escaped his midnight executioners by bribing a jailer with a string of gold pieces.

From the ordeal of his two imprisonments he never recovered. He developed a cough that worsened during the war and carried him to his grave at forty-five.

He left his family an estate of $658,007.43—on the books. In fact, he was bankrupt. The impressive sum was largely the face value of government securities, worth practically nothing. His path led not to glory but to ruin and obscurity. He had walked it knowingly.

There were those, however, who remembered him as long as they lived. The leaders whom he had helped with loans were many and illustrious. Like penniless James Madison, they at first had turned to him reluctantly. They returned in gratitude. The list includes Congressmen Joseph Reed, Arthur Lee, Joseph Jones; Generals St. Clair, Mercer, and Von Steuben ("How can I be inspector general without a decent uniform to wear!"); James Monroe, destined for the presidency; and many more.

From the despised outsider, Haym Salomon rose to be the workhorse of the Treasury, particularly during the impoverished last year of the war, and to paymaster of the French forces in America. When the official counting was made by Congress, it was learned that he had obtained more than six million dollars for the war effort.

Not all the revenue collected in taxes during the Revolution by the thirteen colonies matched the amount raised by Haym Salomon, devout Jew and selfless servant of America.

JOHN ANDRÉ
Rider of the Rainbow

As he rode alone through the no-man's-land above White Plains, Major John André wiggled his toes.

They were cramped and growing numb. His elegant white-topped boots fitted perfectly, for in his appearance as in every beat of his gay, artistic life John André was an Englishman of fashion and refinement.

André's boots pinched for a good reason. Wedged between his feet and stockings rested secret documents written by General Benedict Arnold. They disclosed details for the capture of the rebel fortress at West Point.

Two nights earlier (September 21), André and Arnold had sat together in the darkness of a grove of firs and bargained in half whispers. The dynamic, hawk-nosed general demanded a high price for selling out West Point. The romantic Englishman, a lost child on the pathways of treachery, wavered before the American's furious will.

André allowed himself to be conducted from among the

Born: May 2, 1750, London, England
Died: October 2, 1780, Tappan, N.Y.

firs to the home of Joshua Hett Smith. To his alarm, he found himself within American lines. Arnold glibly pooh-poohed his anxieties. The traitor produced documents which, he said, darkness had prevented his taking to the riverside rendezvous. He urged André to carry the papers back to General Clinton's headquarters. Hesitantly, André agreed.

In gleeful spirits Arnold whirled off to West Point, leaving André stranded. The ship that had brought him up the Hudson had been chased by rebel guns. Faced with a tricky overland journey, André was persuaded by Smith to don one of his long coats.

Almost without realizing it, André had violated three of Clinton's orders—not to stray from neutral ground, not to carry incriminating papers on his person, not to remove his uniform. The discarded warnings were three fingers at his throat.

Nonetheless, John André clung to a belief in the success of his adventure into espionage. He had faith in himself. His genteel talents had easily left behind his nose-to-the-rule-book fellow officers. Indeed, his career owed its twinkling climb entirely to his nonmilitary accomplishments. For a born soldier John André was not.

He had entered the army out of pique. As a youth of nineteen he had stared with dreamy brown eyes from the gloom of a London countinghouse and reflected upon the Muses and a fragile maid of the Midlands. Her hectic coloring had inspired his brush, his pen, and his proposal of marriage. When she jilted him, he hurried off to wars to forget, going first to a humdrum garrison in Germany, then to Canada.

His heart mended better than new. He learned to love not one fair maid but all—including intense Peggy Shippen, Arnold's future bride. As he traveled, he filled a journal with notes and sketches of native flora, fauna, and humans both white and red. General William Howe promoted him to captain—the golden boy of the British army charmed men, too. André returned the favor by staging a fantastic land-and-water party, the *Meschianza*, to honor Sir Billy on his departure for home.

By the time he negotiated in the midnight wood with Arnold, the versatile major had risen to adjutant general of the British army. An early delicacy of face and limb had matured into slender manliness. He was, in the words of a Connecticut militiaman, "the handsomest man I ever laid eyes on."

All the sweets of life were his—if he could safely deliver the papers in his boots. He wanted not Arnold's pot of gold. He rode his own rainbow, one that arched toward honor, fame, and glory. His fine charger bore him past ruined farmhouses and overgrown fields that bespoke the agony which his mission would mercifully terminate. The Tories would reoccupy their estates; the peasants would thrive again under the King.

He approached Tarrytown, far beyond the area reported as dangerous. He had seen neither loyalist cowboys nor rebel skinners, hoodlums whose allegiance was solely to themselves. To his left dipped the lovely vale of Sleepy Hollow. On his right the Hudson River bulged into Tappan Sea. Shortly after nine o'clock he trotted over a creaky little bridge.

A shout, and André beheld three ragged men barring his path. Huge, unwashed John Paulding advanced with firelock pointed at André's chest.

"Gentlemen," said André, smiling, "I hope you belong to my party."

"What party?" asked the big skinner, who was wearing the Hessian coat that he had stolen while escaping from the British a few days before. The coat misled the Englishman, and he answered confidently, "The lower party."

Paulding gave a noncommittal nod, and André babbled on. "I am an officer in the British service out on a particular business. I hope you won't detain me." He pulled out a gold watch, a rarity among poor American officers, to confirm his identity.

Paulding's eyebrows rose. He told the major to dismount. Realizing he had mistaken rebel for loyalist, André nervously forced a laugh. "My God," he blurted. "I must do something to get along!" He showed his pass, signed by Arnold. It permitted him as "John Anderson" to clear the American guards.

Paulding's lips laboriously shaped each word. He looked at the watch and the white-topped boots and again ordered André to dismount. André slid from the saddle protesting.

Beneath a towering tulip tree he was stripped and searched. The highwaymen found no money. Under each foot, however, was a wad of three folded papers. Paulding understood at once.

"My God," he cried. "He's a spy!"

The excited skinners huddled. The gold watch and the expensive boots seemed scarcely worth the risk of being hauled in with a really big fish. They delivered their surprise catch to the American outpost at North Castle.

André felt that his mission, though harassed, was not defeated. His rainbow still reached high into the sky. West Point would fall. Arnold would see that he got back to the British lines.

Benjamin Tallmadge, Washington's Secret Service chief, took him into custody. As the pair rode side by side toward Tappan, André inquired about his prospects. Tallmadge alluded to his Yale classmate, Nathan Hale, hanged as a spy.

"Surely you don't consider his case and mine alike!" André exclaimed.

"They are exactly similar," replied Tallmadge. "And similar will be your fate."

The capture of the comely, talented Englishman dwarfed all other war news. Washington appointed Nathanael Greene to preside over a fourteen-general board of inquiry that included Lafayette, Knox, Glover, and Von Steuben. André believed he must be judged lightly, and he testified with disarming candor. The board was unable to disguise its sorrow in finding him guilty, on his admission.

Washington shocked almost everyone by imposing the death sentence. Benedict Arnold, gone to his purchasers, wrote a scathing letter in which he threatened retaliation "on such unhappy persons of your army as may fall within my power" unless André's life were spared. General Clinton offered to exchange Henry Laurens, former President of Congress imprisoned in the Tower of London, for his agent. Colonel Alexander Hamilton appealed for leniency because "everything that is amiable in virtue, in fortitude, in delicate sentiment and accomplished manners, pleads for him."

Washington refused to be swayed. On October 2, 1780, the day of the execution, André sat in his Tappan room and sketched himself. As he marched out with his guard, he offered compliments on the music of the fife and drums and on the discipline of the troops.

Atop a hillock loomed the gallows. His pleas for a soldier's death by firing squad had been rejected. "Must I die in this manner?" he gasped.

The rainbow was disappearing. Into the dry, rustling past faded the stolen kisses, the scissors quick-clipping silhouettes of pretty girls, the poems "pencill'd unto love."

Many in the crowd of onlookers began to weep as the gentle youth mounted his coffin in the bed of a wagon. He helped the fumbling, face-blackened hangman place the noose around his neck and bind his arms.

General Greene and others who had declared him guilty watched pityingly from horseback. André bowed to them.

"All I request of you gentlemen," he said, "is that you will bear witness to the world that I die like a brave man," and in an undertone, added, "It will be but a momentary pang!"

A blindfold ended sight. A whip slashed. The wagon jerked forward.

For John André, poet, artist, and soldier of misfortune, the rainbow stopped eighteen inches from the ground.

NATHANAEL GREENE

The Complete Soldier

WHEN THE MEN OF THE RHODE ISLAND KENTISH GUARDS prepared to elect officers, they asked themselves the question: Do we want an officer who limps?

It just wouldn't look right for a high-stepping outfit— one of New England's smartest—to have the captain or a lieutenant hobbling at dress reviews.

In October, 1774, the militiamen voted. They voted no— no to Nathanael Greene, who had helped to organize the company.

Nobody knew of a certainty what had caused the stiffness in Greene's right knee. Some claimed it developed in his family's large foundry, where he had to stand on one foot while operating the trip-hammer with the other. More likely, he had hurt the knee on the night he had stolen over the roof to attend a dance in defiance of his Quaker father.

The results of the Kentish Guards election mortified

BORN: July 27, 1742, Potowonmut, R.I.
DIED: June 19, 1786, Mulberry Grove, Ga.

him. Although better qualified than anyone else to be captain, he swallowed his pride and volunteered to serve as a private.

The Rhode Island General Assembly, in which he sat, held a truer opinion of his value. It appointed him to a committee charged with rewriting the military laws of the colony. After the shot heard round the world, the Assembly voted to raise a brigade of fifteen hundred men, and it cast about for a leader.

Chosen was Nathanael Greene, the private in a volunteer company, the broad-shouldered ironmaster of thirty-two years who had never planned or fought a battle, the Quaker who had been read out of the Society of Friends because he believed the American rebellion was "the cause of God and man." A month later, Greene was made brigadier general in the Continental Army.

Another year and he would ascend to major general. Before the peace, he would be hailed on two continents— as the conqueror of the south, as the "strategist of the Revolution," as the man whom Washington wanted as his successor. Such was the acclaim that Nathanael Greene achieved without once being in overall command at a decisive victory.

At first his vast reservoir of talent had to be dripped into the details of preparedness. During the early weeks around Boston, his Rhode Islanders "were the best disciplined and appointed in the whole army." While other militia clapped together shelters of boards, ragged sailcloth, and earth and stone, his men put up a town of orderly tents. Greene constructed redoubts in front of his cannon when little labor was expended elsewhere on fortifications. He had company officers go to general headquarters to learn the correct method of building a stove, because the cooks were wasting fuel and menacing the tents with flying embers.

All his military science Greene had learned from books

and lectures. This lack of war experience may well have worked to his favor. He had no haunting memories to frighten decision into hesitation. He was not controlled by his past, as were Putnam, Ward, and Schuyler. More than any top general, Nathanael Greene was an officer hatched and hardened by the Revolution.

"He came to us the rawest, the most untutored being I ever met with," Henry Knox, another self-educated officer, wrote patronizingly. "But, in less than twelve months, was the equal, in military knowledge, to any General Officer in the army, and very superior to most of them."

In less than twelve months Greene had emerged as the councilor closest to Washington's ear.

Soon, however, other voices were heard. Fort Washington and twenty-eight hundred defenders were captured; in consequence, Fort Lee across the Hudson had to be evacuated. The jealous and discontented whispered that Greene dominated the Commander in Chief. As the broken American army of three thousand straggled across New Jersey, Greene's star verged on eclipse.

He retrieved his prestige in combat. Problems of supply had placed him in Providence on the day of Bunker Hill. Sickness had forced him to relinquish his command before the disaster on Long Island. But on the Christmas night of 1776, he led the left column into Trenton and sealed the defeat of the German detachment.

He of the halting gait covered the retreat after Brandywine and skillfully saved the artillery. And as the wretched Americans struggled into camp at Valley Forge for the winter of 1777-1778, the first of the three phases of Greene's military career closed.

Valley Forge jumped into horrible focus the months of mismanagement in the quartermaster's department. The patriots froze while, as Lafayette described the situation, "hogsheads of shoes, stockings, and clothing were lying at different places on the roads and in the woods, perishing for want of teams, or money to pay the teamsters."

Washington asked Greene to save the situation. Supply had become more essential to survival than a division of regulars. Greene shied from a task without prospect of honor or laurels. "Nobody ever heard of a quartermaster in history," he grumbled. But in March, 1778, he bowed to the desire of his Commander in Chief.

The worst problem, transportation, Greene relieved by building boats, repairing roads, and revising the standards for the purchase of horses. He got the army out of the damp, unhealthful huts and into tents. And for two years, while doubling as strategist and combat leader, he struggled for funds, grasping against the outgoing tide of inflation.

Greene's tenure as quartermaster general, though largely successful, was not altogether sunlit. Like most dedicated Continental officers, he relished wealth. According to the practice, he received a commission of 1 percent of all departmental expenditures. Lamentably, he granted favors to friends, though he stoutly denied wrongdoing. He invested in shipping, real estate, and iron manufacturing. Fate tricked him, and these investments yielded little during his short postwar life.

By the fall of 1780, the war in the north had settled into a watchful stalemate. Washington called once again upon his ablest general to do the seemingly impossible: recover the south.

On December 3 at Charlotte, Greene, the complete soldier, took over the Southern Department from Horatio Gates, who on August 16 had fled the wreckage of his Camden defeat astride a prize racing horse. The third and greatest phase of Greene's military career was begun.

Greene inherited about twenty-five hundred spiritless scarecrows. Without pomp or pretense he went to work rebuilding the army and infusing a fresh sense of patriotism.

After one day, declared Colonel Thomas Polk, he knew more about the supply situation than had Gates in his four months.

The plight of the south strained even Greene's abundant talents. The British ruled the coast, occupied Charleston and Savannah, and controlled the interior by means of a chain of forts. The land itself was ravaged by war, desolate in winter and hot as the "antechamber of hell" in summer. Armed Tories rode vengefully high in the protective shadow of British might.

Outnumbered, Greene adopted guerrilla tactics. Fortunately, he had exactly the right officers: Dan Morgan, the peerless leader of light troops; two slashing cavalrymen, "Light-Horse Harry" Lee and William Washington; and three resilient partisans, Francis Marion, Thomas Sumter, and Andrew Pickens. Most of these difficult, independent men Horatio Gates had failed to use effectively. By tact and by the power of his ability, Nathanael Greene fitted them together and raised triumph from chaos.

His master plan was retreat—and when Cornwallis had followed him too far from his base and had to turn back, Greene turned also and pursued, harassing and punishing.

"The more he is beaten," wrote a British officer, "the farther he advances in the end. He has been indefatigable in collecting troops and leading them to be defeated."

Greene never swallowed the enemy, but he chewed up the British at Guilford Court House, Hobkirk's Hill, Ninety-Six, and Eutaw Springs. A weary, exasperated Cornwallis quit North Carolina and retired to his doom at Yorktown. The remaining Redcoats under Alexander Leslie fled to Charleston, where Greene had them besieged when hostilities ceased.

A grateful south lavished gifts upon him. South Carolina gave him an estate of seven thousand acres. North Carolina contributed twenty-five thousand acres along the Cumberland River. Georgia added two thousand acres of excellent rice lands.

The ironmaster whom the Kentish Guards rejected as a company officer could step from any one of the three elegant homes at which it pleased him to sojourn, and wander through gorgeous plantation gardens, limping slightly.

FRANCIS MARION

Swamp Fox

I*N THE HOME OF* C*APTAIN* A*LEXANDER* M*c*Q*UEEN,* REBEL officers relaxed from the daytime chore of fortifying Charleston. As goblets rose and tipped in praise of liberty, Lieutenant Colonel Francis Marion began to look for a way out.

The British were already perched on the seaboard islands, prepared for their second thrust against the south. Marion had no intention of losing his wits for a single night.

Withdrawing from the residence of the commanding general's adjutant, however, presented a delicate problem in tactics. McQueen had locked the doors till justice was rendered to his stock of spirits. Quietly Marion deserted the table and sauntered upstairs. He opened a window and decamped.

The fall to the ground broke his ankle. When word of the injury spread through Charleston, most people thought him a great fool for his pains. Few perceived the obvious:

B*ORN:* ca. 1732, St. John's Parish, S.C.
D*IED:* February 26, 1795, Pond Bluff, S.C.

Francis Marion was an officer who could not be kept where he did not care to stay.

The broken ankle proved to be a blessing in disguise. Unfit for duty, Marion departed from Charleston on a litter. While he hid with friends along the Santee, Sir Henry Clinton captured Charleston, bagging General Benjamin Lincoln's fifty-five hundred Continentals and militia, valuable stores, and most of the South Carolina patriot navy. With the capital in his control, Clinton turned his Redcoats to the conquest of the state.

Congress gave General Horatio Gates, the bogus hero of Saratoga, an army of three thousand and sent him to the rescue. Gates called for every soldier in South Carolina who had escaped capture to rally to him.

Marion responded on a swollen ankle. Amused snickers greeted his arrival in the Continental camps. His crimson coat and blue breeches were shabby. His round leather helmet was scorched on one side, and the tarnished silver crescent in front bearing the inscription "Liberty or Death" (the motto of his regiment) lent him an air of comic bravado.

Some officers hazily recalled the name . . . Marion. He had served five useful if unspectacular years. Now he was commandant of the Second Regiment of South Carolina—or had been. His regiment had surrendered to Clinton.

A commander without a command. The Continental Army sagged with his kind.

A few bedraggled refugees from the Second Regiment drifted into camp. Some twenty mounted followers, both black and white, collected about Marion.

The appearance of the wretchedly equipped band of state troops, wrote Gates's adjutant, "was so burlesque that it was with much difficulty that the diversion of the regular soldiery was restrained by the officers."

The soldiers who had laughed at the first sight of the little French Huguenot watched him with nagging curiosity. He was forty-eight, wizened, and walked with a swaying limp. He had an eagle nose and beady black eyes that peered relentlessly. Spelling and grammar troubled him. He spoke seldom, but when he did, his followers heeded.

Marion was a man of action, and the role of spare officer taxed his patience. He went to Gates and requested permission to ride below Camden and take over the Williamsburg militia. Reinforced, he could burn boats useful to the Redcoats and gather intelligence on troop movements.

Gates gladly detached the scrawny little officer. On August 15, 1780, Francis Marion and his men rode toward the interior of South Carolina and their destiny as partisans.

Two days later Marion was burning scows and flats at the ferries when some Whigs found him. They carried shocking news. Cornwallis had demolished Gates near Camden. In an offshoot of the catastrophe, the guerrilla bivouac of Thomas Sumter had been cut to pieces by Banastre Tarleton. Sumter, the reckless "Carolina Gamecock," had beaten for Charlotte.

South Carolina lay prostrate. In March the state assembly had adjourned in the face of British invasion to meet no more for two years. Governor John Rutledge had quit the capital in April. There was no civil government, and Cornwallis and Tarleton had violently reduced the Southern Department of the American Army to a name on paper.

Francis Marion suddenly was stranded as the senior officer of South Carolina, a state in which the British backed by powerful Tory forces seemed unshakably enthroned.

The only resistance possible, Marion realized, lay in guerrilla warfare. The requisites were twofold: courage and instinct. Marion had both.

At raiding enemy outposts and supply trains, at bush-whacking enemy patrols, and at freeing prisoners—in the swiftness of decision and movement that straightens strategy into simple intuition—the wiry little man in the beat-up leather helmet was to show himself second to none.

He cleared Robert McLeroth out of Williamsburg, de-feated John Watson's Regiment of Guards, drove Lord Rawdon half crazy, and caused Cornwallis, recovering from malaria, to take a personal hand in guiding Tarleton in the drive to hunt him down.

"This damned old Fox, the devil himself could not catch him!" cried Tarleton when once Marion eluded him in Ox Swamp. The Whigs along the Santee altered and shortened Tarleton's description to "Swamp Fox." The title fitted him, and it stuck.

The biggest weapons in the Swamp Fox's arsenal were cunning and stealth. All eastern Carolina became his private hunting grounds. His hideouts were spongy islands among swamps reeking with rotting vegetation and draped by mists and snakes and Spanish moss. From his favorite lairs at Snow's Island or Pyre's Plantation he crept by night. With sharp teeth he ripped at the British and terrorized the large population of Tories between the Santee and the Little Pee Dee Rivers. Then, before sunset, he and his men slipped back along secret trails, leaving their pursuers to flounder in muck and jungle.

The exasperated Colonel Watson complained: "They will not fight like gentlemen. But like savages are eternally firing and whooping around us by night, and by day way-laying and popping at us from behind every tree."

The size of Marion's band varied from foray to foray, from a handful to a few hundred. Under South Carolina law, militia served only thirty days. During times when their families and farms were not endangered, the men cantered home. Marion was left desperately shorthanded.

The men came back, most of them, again and again. Back to the bayous and bogs, the withering heat, the dread malaria-carrying anopheline mosquitoes. They wore home-spun and raided for horses and saddles and bridles. They ate sweet potatoes and pork and corn bread, and did with-out a surgeon and medicine.

For two years they followed the homely little man who swigged nothing stronger than a mixture of vinegar and water, ate from a bark plate, and never seemed to tire. They rode without much expectation of reward. Marion shared their hardships and protected them from foolish risks. Astride a sorrel gelding he had named Ball (after John Ball, a defeated foe and the animal's original owner), he violated flags of truce, shot from ambush, and kept alive patriot resistance within the tight fist of the British.

When the American army under Nathanael Greene moved into South Carolina, Brigadier General Marion's aid was quickly enlisted. Although jealous of his inde-pendent militia command, he did vital outpost duty for "Light-Horse Harry" Lee.

In his willingness to cooperate, Marion confirmed his value above other partisan leaders of the south. Andrew Pickens, a dour man, rarely bothered to account for his movements. Thomas Sumter possessed too much self-interest to work in with grand strategy.

Within two months of a redoubled American offensive, the interior British forts were taken. Marion helped capture Fort Watson and Fort Motte. The Redcoats retired to Charleston, whence they eventually sailed for England.

Marion's partisans disbanded by squads in swamps, under giant cypress trees, and among yellow jessamine and gallberry. The Swamp Fox conducted his last muster at Fair Lawn. After a simple speech, he reined Ball's head for Pond Bluff, a plantation on the Santee he had purchased before the war. He died there at sixty-three.

The places where he rode as a partisan leader are almost without number. The names fall quaintly on modern ears: Wibo Swamp, Tearcoat, Sampit River, Black Mingo, Lower Bridge.

Wherever his night riders galloped—Fish Dam Creek, Wahee Neck, Halfway Swamp, Catfish Creek—ghostly hoofbeats seem still to pound, stirring a page in the legend of the Swamp Fox.

HENRY LEE
Light-Horse Harry

On a raw February afternoon in 1781 a column of
Americans broke out of a straggly forest in North Carolina
and marched southward across an unplowed meadow.

In the center of the cavalry section rode two British
officers. They sat their saddles tensely. Five American
pistols were pointed at their hearts.

In the lead rode a lieutenant colonel of twenty-five years
—well-bred, quick-witted, and cold-blooded. He was
Henry Lee, already known as "Light-Horse Harry" for his
sure, sometimes savage, command of horse.

The previous month he had seized Georgetown, South
Carolina, with Francis Marion's irregulars. The garrison
had eluded them by retreating to the safety of the fort.
Now Lee was hunting a man who didn't run from a fight—
Banastre Tarleton, the "British Attila."

Lee had got wind that Tarleton was camped nearby
with a large troop of cavalry, two brass cannon, and four

Born: January 29, 1756, Leesylvania, Va.
Died: March 25, 1818, Cumberland Island, Ga.

hundred infantry. But the British camp was found deserted except for the two officers. Tarleton, a new intelligence reported, was preparing to camp six miles farther on.

Taking the two Redcoats prisoner, Lee had conceived a bold hoax. All the south was torn by partisan warfare between ununiformed loyalists and ununiformed rebels. In order to surprise Tarleton, Lee planned to pass as either British or Continental troops, depending on who was encountered.

The column had just struck a dirt road when two young farmers rode into view and reined up uncertainly. Lee measured their hesitation. Pretending to be reinforcements for Tarleton from Hillsborough, he hailed them in a cordial voice.

The two farmers expressed relief. They had been dispatched to locate Tarleton's camp and to lead Colonel John Pyle and his four hundred loyalists there.

Lee saluted the brave youths. With a friendly smile he apologized for a slight interruption. He spoke quietly to his adjutant. The officer galloped back to Colonel Andrew Pickens, whose irregulars had been temporarily attached to Lee's Legion. Pickens was ordered to drift his riflemen into the woods on the left of the road.

The pair of captive British officers glared at the pistols trained on them. To expose the plot meant instant death.

Lee sprinkled praise over the farmers for joining Cornwallis. He directed one of them back to Colonel Pyle with the suggestion that he pull his loyalists to the side of the road for the cavalry to pass. He sent, too, the greetings of Lieutenant Colonel Tarleton.

Presently the Legion reached the loyalists, dutifully drawn up in single rank along the edge of the road to Lee's right. They bestrode their horses proudly, rifles or muskets slung comfortably over their shoulders.

Colonel Pyle was at the far end, an ideal position. Lee

intended to draw up his cavalry, the core of his Legion, facing the amateurs. He would offer Pyle the chance to disband his men or enlist them in General Nathanael Greene's army.

As he rode along, Lee nodded approvingly. His compliments upon their smart, soldierly appearance left the defenders of the King flushed with self-esteem. He stopped by Colonel Pyle and the two men shook hands.

Pyle had no reason to suspect deception. The Legion in short, bright green jackets resembled the famed Green Dragoons of Tarleton. And certainly this blue-eyed officer with his powdered blond hair tied in a sleek queue, his polished boots and lambskin breeches, his helmet topped by a white horsehair plume—certainly he had the formidable demeanor of a professional soldier, a British soldier.

Suddenly the make-believe shattered. Lee dropped Pyle's hand.

Pickens' militia had come up but had been spotted through the trees on the other side of the road. A few loyalists fired point-blank into the Legion right before them. The other loyalists were still clumsily unslinging their weapons when sabers flashed. Pistols discharged at a range that left powder burns on ninety loyalist corpses.

Colonel Pyle was left for dead. Almost all the loyalists were killed or hacked horribly by Lee's veterans. Tarleton, warned by the noisy affray, broke camp. Before Lee could close, the British cavalryman had been ordered to rejoin Cornwallis. Lee was summoned back by Greene to act as a guard between him and the enemy.

The massacre, coupled with a dogged American offense to recapture the south, shook the stoutest loyalists in North Carolina. Cornwallis, who had counted heavily on their military support, found instead fear or indifference.

As for Lee, he was more disturbed at booting the opportunity to engage Tarleton than by the slaughter at the roadside. Hence the grisly episode has importance apart from the military. It catches fast the character of America's ablest Revolutionary cavalryman.

Ingenuity, a fervor for secrecy, and the zeal to seek out a fight characterized "Light-Horse Harry" Lee throughout his service.

A nonrelation, General Charles Lee, said of him that he was so adept in war that he seemed "to have sprung out of his mother's womb a soldier."

A prize tribute, but hardly accurate. Henry sprang from a family that had been illustrious Virginia planters for a century before his birth at Leesylvania, his father's sprawling home. His mother, Lucy Grymes, was young Colonel George Washington's first unrequited love.

At seventeen Henry graduated from the College of New Jersey (now Princeton), having shown talent in Latin. With hosts of slaves to do the work, the youth passed his time in preparing to study law in England. His only grounding for warfare was the horsemanship he practiced astride the blooded steeds of his father's stables. A muscular dandy in plum-colored breeches, ruffles, and lace, he never missed a ball. He interspersed a keen game of cards between minuets, jigs, marches, and country reels.

With the outbreak of war, Henry, nineteen, rode from Leesylvania to Washington's army with a commission as captain in the Virginia Light Dragoons. Leading the First Troop, he quickly displayed outstanding skill at foraging, skirmishing, and reconnaissance.

In April, 1778, Lee was promoted to the rank of major and placed in command of three troops of cavalry and three companies of infantry. Known as "Lee's Legion," the men had the stirring look of seasoned soldiers in their tall caps draped with bearskin, their short green jackets and white linen breeches. Under Lee's leadership they fought as well as they looked. The Legion became the trouble-shooting unit of the Continental Army.

Washington warmed to the enterprising youth and in-

vited him to headquarters as an aide. Lee declined this
high honor, despite its comforts, safety, and the enviable
companionship of the army's foremost officers.

"I am wedded to my sword," he wrote. "My secondary
object in this present war is military reputation."

Far from feeling slighted, Washington assured the young
warrior of his good opinion. A lifetime friendship formed
between the two men.

With the Legion a semi-independent force, Lee had the
vehicle to quest for liberty according to his own ideas.
Always in the forefront of his thinking was secrecy.

Reconnoitering for Wayne's surprise attack on Stony
Point, Lee ensured secrecy by killing all dogs in the
neighborhood. He also caught and hanged a deserter from
the First Regiment and sent his head back to camp as a
warning. He appalled Washington by urging that all
deserters be treated in a like manner.

Since he took no part in the storming of Stony Point, Lee
added little to his cherished "military reputation." He
determined, therefore, to emulate the feat on his own. He
selected Paulus Hook, opposite New York City, for the
monument to himself. Four days after Stony Point, he
captured it in a brilliant victory that fell short of Wayne's
only in the number of troops involved.

When the war moved south he wrested British forts in
South Carolina (with Francis Marion) and in Georgia.
His daring and ingenuity served him masterfully. To reduce
Fort Watson he built a log tower from which his marksmen
could fire into the stockade. He burned out the defenders
of Fort Motte by shooting flaming arrows into the principal
building. He won Fort Granby without bloodshed by terrifying the commander with a show of bayonets. He sucked
the enemy out of Fort Galphin with a fake attack and took
the stronghold with his main force. He conquered Fort
Grierson by an assault that fanned into a vendetta. He

captured Fort Cornwallis by siege. Later, he probably saved the drawn battle of Eutaw Springs from becoming an American defeat.

He witnessed Cornwallis' surrender at Yorktown. With his native state free, he quit the army to wed a cousin, Matilda Lee. After her death he remarried. The fifth child of this second marriage was Robert E. Lee.

Half a century later Robert was to bring to fruition that tree of "military reputation" which "Light-Horse Harry" had so fiercely planted for the Lees of Virginia in the soil of America.

DANIEL MORGAN

Hercules in Fringed Leather

Pickets brought Brigadier General Daniel Morgan the news. Banastre Tarleton, the dreaded "British Attila," had picked up his trail.

Big Dan Morgan knew his peril. The rough-and-tumble life of the Virginia frontier had seasoned him in the ways of men and war. A place must be found to stand and fight. Caught unprepared, his one-thousand-man force invited the merciless sabering of "Tarleton's Quarter."

In spite of the danger, Morgan held his mount to a walk. The raw air gouged at his rheumatism and made unbearable a faster gait across the bog holes and creeks of upper South Carolina.

Winter had pared the countryside to a wasteland denuded of food and forage. Few of the weary, hungry men would have long followed another leader on anything so aimless as this mission. The previous month Nathanael Greene, newly commanding in the south, had given

Born: 1736, Hunterdon County (?), N.J.
Died: July 6, 1802, Winchester, Va.

Morgan a mixed force and wandering orders. The "Hercules in fringed leather," only recently returned from sulking retirement, was to collect militia, and protect and "spirit up" the people of the western Carolinas.

Greene's act of dividing his outnumbered army into two parts had at first perplexed his adversary, Cornwallis. The English earl had countered by going one better. He had split his army in three. One contingent he had sent to secure Camden. The second he had himself led north after Greene. The third he had placed under the "invincible" Banastre Tarleton with instructions to track down Morgan and destroy him.

Morgan doubled his patrols and set in motion a grim, two-day contest of hide-and-seek. His Welsh temper rose with each retreating step, and he scanned the slopes and fields impatiently for the right spot. In the rainy twilight of January 16, 1781, his blue eyes measured a rolling area five miles wide and five miles deep.

It was Hannah's Cowpens, so called after the man who had once pastured cattle there. The Cowpens . . .

Here is the spot, Morgan told his officers. Here we turn and fight.

The officers stared in dismay. Two hills, one behind the other, crowned a grassy slope. Both front and flanks were bare of ridges, thickets, or swamps along which to stake a battle line or defend against cavalry (Tarleton's horse outnumbered Morgan's three to one). Six miles to the rear flowed the muddy, virtually unfordable Broad River, cutting off escape in case of defeat.

In the very weaknesses of Cowpens, Morgan perceived its subtle advantages. He trusted his officers and his regulars, but not the militia, who by night comprised about half his manpower.

Morgan did not want a swamp in full view of the militia: they would bolt for it at the first shot. As to protecting his flanks, he knew Tarleton and was confident he'd have nothing save head-on fighting. As to retreat—he wanted to kill all hope of *that*.

"When men are forced to fight, they will sell their lives dearly," he asserted afterward. "And I knew that the dread of Tarleton's cavalry would give us due weight to the protection of my bayonets and keep my troops from breaking. . . . Had I crossed the river, one half of my militia would immediately have abandoned me."

That night Morgan wasted no time on sleep. He received the local militia who continued to arrive. He walked among his men, helped them fix bayonets, kidded about their sweethearts, and promised to crack the whip over cocksure Ban Tarleton.

A former waggoner, Dan Morgan knew about whips. He knew, too, about hard fighting, any style.

His muscular body bore scars that read like chapters of his forty-five years of life. One of his toes was bent out of place, broken while kicking an opponent during a fistfight long, long ago. The gash on his left cheek recalled a bullet wound suffered during a hairbreadth escape from an Indian ambush. The 499 stripes on his broad back were inflicted at the order of an enraged British subaltern whom Waggoner Morgan had knocked cold with a brawny fist.

On Revolutionary battlegrounds—Boston, Quebec, New Jersey, Saratoga—the Redcoats learned to respect Morgan and his buckskin-clad sharpshooters. Their long rifles, which killed at twice the range of muskets, were dubbed "the most fatal widow-and-orphan-makers in the world."

The cold, scared Americans at Cowpens took heart from such a leader. Morgan understood them, for he had often experienced fear, though never cowardice. And he recognized his own shortcomings. The aristocratic inner circle of the army regarded him as a primeval outsider. With the

quiet help of his wife, he was to smoothen the roughhewn
edges till in future days he could stand at ease in the halls
of Congress.

The word came in the pitch darkness before dawn.
Tarleton was five miles away and driving.

"Boys, get up!" Morgan bellowed. "Benny's coming!"

Calmly he let his men eat breakfast before deploying
them in four lines.

In the front he posted one hundred and fifty militia as
skirmishers, about a yard apart. Some one hundred and
fifty yards behind on the slope, he strung out three hundred
militia at the same interval. Behind them on the summit of
the first hill he placed his main line, four hundred and
fifty Continental light infantry. Behind the second hill, out
of sight, he stationed Colonel William Washington's eighty
dragoons and forty-five infantrymen who had volunteered
to ride as cavalry.

Morgan rode along his first line and spoke in a fatherly
tone to the men. Let the enemy come within fifty yards,
fire two rounds—aiming at the men with epaulets—and
retire into the spaces of the second line. The militia would
run anyway, and Morgan wanted to show them how to
retreat without panic. The second line was to fire as long
as possible, fall back, and become the reserve behind
the Continentals.

The scheme, calling for the weakest units to take the
first shock, was new and original. Would it work? Dawn
brought the answer in a stirring among the trees across the
gentle valley—Tarleton.

The British formed hurriedly: Legion infantry in the
center, dragoons on both flanks, kilted Highlanders and
cavalry in reserve. The movements were beautiful to behold, a colorful overture to this classic meeting of the tall
frontiersman and the stocky, Oxford-educated young
hotspur.

Tarleton gloated. The Americans had not eluded him across the river!

In numbers the opposing sides were nearly equal. But the British held the advantage in the only cannon—two 3-pounders—and in trained regulars. Hotly eager, Tarleton attacked.

The two American militia lines fired steadily and then peeled off to the rear, according to plan. At this seeming retreat, the British rushed forward over their own dead. Suddenly the withdrawing militia uncovered the Continental line, muskets blazing. American and British regulars gunned each other in thirty minutes of fighting as brave as any in the war.

Morgan's novel mousetrap pattern was developing perfectly when suddenly an order was misunderstood on the right. The Continentals there turned and walked to the rear.

Tarleton screamed jubilantly of a rout. His Redcoats tore into the opening like a wild mob, up the first hill and down the back slope.

Cool and steady, Morgan met the crisis. "Face about!" he roared. "Give them one fire and the day is ours!"

The Continentals wheeled in their tracks. There was no time to aim with the British thundering down on them.

The Americans fired from the hip at forty yards—and followed with the bayonet. Then, with the timing of clockwork, the militia, having re-formed out of sight, struck the British left flank.

The tired, bewildered Redcoats, slashed by Washington's cavalry, ripped by muskets, rifles, and bayonets, surrendered wholesale.

Tarleton pulled his surviving horsemen in flight. Behind him he left the flower of Cornwallis' light troops and his own reputation for invincibility.

While a nation rejoiced, aching Dan Morgan took his

mud-splashed little army north to a reunion with Greene. Soon afterward illness forced his retirement, though he reappeared briefly to assist Lafayette in Virginia.

Far away, Congress voted a gold medal to the indomitable Old Waggoner whose mastery of a fantastic hour of fighting on a patch of grazing land forged the first link in the long chain that ended at Yorktown.

CHARLES CORNWALLIS

No Ending at Yorktown

THE FIRST STREETS WERE LAID OUT IN 1691 OVERLOOKING the York River. From that year forward the destiny of Yorktown was shaped on the water.

By the middle of the eighteenth century the Virginia town had reached the height of its prosperity. Some one thousand people dwelt on or about the stone-marl bluffs. Fortunes were made in tobacco.

Then the surrounding soil began wearing thin. New ports vied for every hogshead of freight. Whole families moved away, and slowly the vigor waned.

After 1750, Yorktown began to slide back.

And on an October day in 1781, the clock stopped altogether.

The man who worked the miracle—who embalmed an entire town for generations of American sightseers—was a beefy, red-faced lieutenant general, Earl Charles Cornwallis, since April, 1778, second-in-command of the

BORN: December 31, 1738, Grosvenor Square, England
DIED: October 5, 1805, Ghazipore, India

British army in America. Haughty in manner and overbold in combat, he disliked the inactivity of garrison posts. He never saw Yorktown in a very favorable light.

But he had orders from General Clinton, the Commander in Chief. Cornwallis knew how to unpack his orders and to wear them like blinkers when the going flitted distractingly all over the landscape. Since he had entered Virginia in May, he had been futilely chasing the butterfly Lafayette. He had finally transferred his troops to Yorktown in August, having become "quite tired of marching about the country in quest of adventures."

A Captain galloped across the level, scrubby fields. He reported that the Yorktown militia, three hundred strong, had fled toward Williamsburg without firing a shot.

Cornwallis established headquarters in the fine home of Thomas Nelson, Sr., a former secretary of the colony. That night he slept soundly. His conscience was clear, for he enjoyed the imperious attitude of the aristocrat toward the struggles and bloodletting of the populace.

Yorktown, as he found it on his morning inspection, was a good soldiers' town. Along the waterfront numerous drinking and lodging places intermingled with wharves and warehouses. In the town proper stood the larger homes, inns, shops, churches, and public buildings of the county. The majority of the houses were of brick, giving the provincial little settlement an air of amusing pretentiousness in the eyes of the British Earl.

After a lunch of far-famed York River oysters, he relaxed. If things turned out badly here, the blame must land upon Clinton. As for himself, he would scarcely break stride on the long highway of his career.

Clinton had decided that a Chesapeake base was necessary. He had wanted a site that could be defended by its garrison and yet protect a fleet anchorage. Alas, being in

New York, he had worded his orders in a vague and general way.

How big a garrison had he in mind? And where was this ideal site—this North American Gibraltar?

The saddlesore Cornwallis, panting from his butterfly chase through Virginia, had grabbed at the loopholes in the orders. Ignoring the chance to net Lafayette, he had backed *all* his weary troops into the best rest-camp-by-the-sea he could find, Yorktown.

He dug in immediately. No one could accuse Lord Cornwallis of not being well trained.

"Nothing but hard labor goes on here at present in constructing and making Batteries toward the River and Redoubts toward the Land," wrote a British soldier on August 31. A double line of fortifications took shape. The main line of ten redoubts and fourteen batteries hugged the town; the outer line followed the natural protective features of creeks and ravines.

To help the gunners aim the sixty-five pieces of artillery, all trees and buildings were knocked down for a thousand yards in front of the main line. The sandy soil, which had disheartened so many tobacco farmers, favored the Redcoats. With a mere four hundred entrenching tools for more than six thousand troops, the easy digging was a blessing.

When completed, the fortifications would do against the forty-five hundred troops of Lafayette and Wayne, Cornwallis believed. After all, the British position at Yorktown depended on water, not upon land, and His Majesty's navy ruled the waves. The royal ships of war could either sustain Cornwallis indefinitely or evacuate him for consolidation in New York. The choice was Clinton's.

Suddenly, incredibly, the choice belonged to the allies.

"The enemy's fleet has returned," Cornwallis wrote. "Two line-of-battleships and one frigate lie at the mouth of this river. . . . I hear Washington arrived. . . . my half unfinished works . . ."

Although aware that overwhelming allied armies were assembling against him, Cornwallis stayed aloof behind his blinkers. He did nothing through September to smash out while the enemy forces were still divided. He knew how war looked at home, where careers were made or unmade.

He understood the nuances of defeat: the loser on the open field is always suspect of bad generalship, whereas the loser of a siege may often be applauded for his gallant defense. Having advanced his army career largely by purchase, having matured in politics rather than in war, Earl Cornwallis was not about to stub his toe upon a cementy little town in the wilds of Virginia.

Enemy sappers and miners laid out laths of pine end to end upon a line marked by engineers for trenches. The first allied siege line, intended to bring men and artillery within firing range of the British, progressed steadily despite Cornwallis' guns.

For a time the British artillery boomed unopposed. But a sobered Cornwallis watched the allied siege line strangling him. On the night of September 16-17, he wrote Clinton: "If you cannot relieve me very soon, you must be prepared to hear the worst."

The allies began moving up artillery from landing places on the James River.

Clinton sent back word. A relief expedition would sail from New York on October 5.

Cornwallis received this intelligence on September 29, and that night he withdrew his men from the still incomplete outer line. Clinton had shepherded him into this predicament; Clinton must get him out. No foolhardy stand behind inadequate works was going to chip the porcelain-like record of Charles Cornwallis, future Lord Lieutenant of Ireland and Governor General of India.

The first allied siege line was completed October 6. Shortly after three P.M. on October 9 the allied artillery barrage of fifty-two guns was opened by the French. The cannonading continued until resistance ceased eight days after.

The devastation was horrible. "The inhabitants of the city fled with their belongings to the river and hid themselves on the hillside in sand and rocks," wrote a German mercenary. "Still they did not entirely escape, for many of them were fatally injured through the ricocheting of the bombs . . ."

Red-hot shot ignited the heavily tarred British ships in the harbor. Cornwallis' headquarters along with many other buildings were demolished. Narrowly missing death, the Earl removed to a sturdy brick building farther within the town.

All seemed lost, and yet the etiquette of combat required one last gesture. On the night of October 16–17, he sent picked troops across the river to Gloucester Point, held by Banastre Tarleton, to probe the chance of breaking through for a sprint northward. A midnight storm upset the boats. Having made the gesture, he recalled the troops that had crossed safely.

The allies had captured redoubts nine and ten, finishing their second siege line, and they hunkered within storming distance. The Earl's men were deserting in droves. None of his guns operated. Food was down to putrid meat and stony biscuits.

Clinton's relief force had failed to appear. The situation, Cornwallis saw, was hopelessly against him.

He took council with his officers probably in a cave near the water. At ten o'clock on the morning of October 17, 1781, an officer and a drummer boy in red climbed upon a parapet. The officer waved a white cloth through the battle haze. The drummer boy beat resolutely to a parley.

Lord Cornwallis, the apotheosis of the conventional eighteenth-century gentleman-soldier, had put up the gallant defense that convention demanded.

. England, a forgiving nation, would send him to India to thrash the Tippo Sahib, to France to negotiate the Treaty of Amiens with Napoleon's brother Joseph, to Ireland to suppress rebellion. And as he floated on the Ganges in a state barge, or sat in Dublin Castle, or strolled in the shadows of Amiens Cathedral, he had an occasional dim memory.

It was of a used-up little tobacco town in whose burned-out soil he had buried his most artful triumph.

The escape from disgrace.

FRANÇOIS DE GRASSE

Le Coup de Grasse

IN ORDINARY TIMES FRENCH ADMIRAL FRANÇOIS JOSEPH Paul de Grasse stood six feet two inches tall; but under fire, his sailors insisted, he towered six feet six inches.

De Grasse seemed to sprout those gallant, danger-fed four inches on the day he brought his fleet to the island of Saint Domingue and dropped anchor off Cape Français, the Paris of the West Indies. Awaiting him were three letters from his countryman Count Rochambeau, who commanded the French troops under Washington. Rochambeau painted a dark picture: the American cause after six years of war was collapsing from exhaustion.

The first of Rochambeau's letters avowed that the arrival of a French fleet would "save this situation"; it recommended an attack either at Chesapeake Bay, Virginia, or at New York. The second letter disclosed that the French military chest held funds to support the army only until August 20, a month away; it requested 1,200,000

BORN: 1722, Bar-sur-Loup, France
DIED: January 14, 1788, Paris, France

silver livres. The third letter cried for more troops: "Four or five thousand men will not be too many."

Raise money, bring troops, decide on the point of attack, and gain superiority of the seas!

No man, not even George Washington, had been called upon to interweave so many feats so rapidly. If the tall French nobleman failed, the Continental Army might die here and there, muskets stacked in fields and earthworks from Bunker Hill to Savannah.

The odds seemed overwhelmingly against the sixty-year-old Count de Grasse. The West Indies fleet, awarded him four months earlier, was his first flag command. He was a product—at best a skilled one—of a decaying eighteenth-century naval system whereby family rank obtained more promotions than did achievement. A further weakness, perfected by the French, lurked in the training program. Artistic maneuvering was stressed over sheer hard fighting. When the French navy did engage, it was with the philosophy of risking much for defense and of attacking only if the risk was scant.

De Grasse read and reread Rochambeau's letters before making up his mind. The southwesterly winds and the distress of the southern states decided for Chesapeake Bay. From there he needed only two days to reach New York.

The soldiers, next. Three French regiments from the Saint Domingue garrison had been transferred to Spanish Admiral Don Josef Solano for an expedition against Florida. Since Solano did not wish to embark until winter, de Grasse borrowed them back—three thousand infantrymen, one hundred artillerymen, one hundred dragoons, ten field cannon, and some mortars and siege guns.

Next, the raising of 1,200,000 livres in cash. Although he was descended from one of the oldest noble families in France, although he possessed enormous charm and

prestige, rebuff met him everywhere. As security for the
loan to the French King, he pledged his estate in France
and his plantations on the island. One of his captains also
pledged his plantation. The worth of these properties ex-
ceeded the sum desired, but the offers were refused. In
desperation, de Grasse talked the Spanish director of
customs into an attempt at raising the money in Havana.
De Grasse hopefully dispatched frigate *Aigrette* to take the
money on board.

With the troops collected and his ships provisioned, de
Grasse did not delay over the money. On July 28, 1781, he
sent frigate *Concorde* with a letter to Rochambeau stating
that he was coming—to Chesapeake Bay. On August 5,
his fleet slipped cables and put to sea. The wide-flung pieces
of the task he had undertaken three weeks before began to
drop in place and acquire the shape of a master stroke.

From his station aboard his flagship, *Ville de Paris*, one
of the mightiest ships afloat on the oceans of the world, de
Grasse steered for the Old Channel between Cuba and the
Bahama Banks. By taking this longer, stormy route,
"where no fleet ever passed," he aimed to hide his where-
abouts from the British.

British Admiral George Rodney heard of the French
fleet's departure, but he could not believe that de Grasse
was taking *all* his ships, leaving the French sugar islands
defenseless. He ordered Samuel Hood north from the
Indies with fourteen ships. Following the regular route,
Hood bowled unknowingly past the French. He reached
Chesapeake Bay first, found it vacant, and continued on to
New York where, mystified, he joined his superior, Admiral Thomas Graves.

By then *Aigrette* had returned to de Grasse. She carried
the 1,200,000 livres, raised within a few hours in Havana.
On August 30, the fleet skimmed into Chesapeake Bay like
swallows of hope. Troops and guns were landed at James

Town and united with the commands of Lafayette and Wayne to block the escape of Cornwallis from Yorktown into North Carolina.

Cornwallis had encamped at Yorktown eight days earlier under cloudy orders from Sir Henry Clinton to take a strong position that could guard a fleet anchorage. Yorktown appeared a reasonable site. Only suddenly the ships at anchor were the comely black hulls of the enemy. And Washington and Rochambeau were hastening south in a fury of joy to tighten the trap by land.

Yet this masterpiece of timing and strategy, this merging of the forces of two nations on land and sea, still trembled on an *if*.

If de Grasse could defeat the British fleet and so maintain the blockade of Cornwallis . . .

On September 5, the *if* sprang into the morning sky above Cape Henry. The British fleet of nineteen ships of the line under Graves had been sighted. De Grasse sailed out with twenty-four ships to give fight.

For five agonizing days independence dangled blindly while the fleets battled out of sight beyond the horizon. Previous French naval cooperation (under excuse-ridden Count Charles d'Estaing) had been tormentingly futile. A British victory now meant that Cornwallis could be safely removed or reinforced from the water. The cost of transferring the armies of Washington and Rochambeau from New York to Yorktown would be a bankrupting waste.

The battle was decided the first day. De Grasse, standing six feet six inches, had a position to defend, and in the best tradition of the French navy, he risked everything. After a successful opening, in which no ships were sunk, he maneuvered Graves away from the capes. Finding the coast clear, the French squadron under Count Louis de Barras running from Newport ducked into Chesapeake Bay. Besides eight ships and four frigates, de Barras brought eighteen transports loaded with salt meat and the French heavy ordnance.

With perfect timing, de Grasse outraced the Royal navy back to the bay. Bolstered by de Barras' squadron, he massed too stout a line for the timid Graves to dispute. The English ships headed back to New York.

The series of naval actions, lumped together as the Battle of the Virginia Capes, wear no patina of drama or splendor. The British were handicapped by petty jealousy, indecision, and a new system of signals that miscarried. Battles and heroes, however, become important only by the verdict of results. What the aristocratic Count de Grasse won was all-important—supremacy in the middle Atlantic long enough for Cornwallis to decide rescue by sea was impossible. Outnumbered and trapped by French and Americans on land, he surrendered. With his army fell the British desire to continue the costly war.

Still, victory had been snatched by the closest of margins. On October 19, Graves had sailed from New York with twenty-five ships and seven thousand men intended for the relief of Yorktown. En route he had learned of the surrender but sailed on. After several days of trying to lure de Grasse out to battle, he returned dolefully to New York.

Despite Washington's plea that he stay, de Grasse sailed under orders for the West Indies and his winter quarters. He overcame British Admiral Samuel Hood, but in April engaged crusty Admiral Rodney. Off Saints Passage, Rodney turned his ships to fighting, not maneuvering. He scattered the French fleet and took de Grasse prisoner.

Like all defeated leaders during the Revolution, de Grasse was lionized by his captors. In London the royal family flattered him and everybody seemed eager to alibi his defeat. The English could afford such chivalry. Rodney's victory restored Britain's control of the seas and steeled her hand at the peace table.

De Grasse' welcome in France was different. He found himself the scapegoat for the humiliation of the outmoded French navy. He went quickly into retirement.

France forgot the Count, for the days of his greatness were short and they belonged to a grateful people far across the Atlantic.

Not until 1931 was a statue of him dedicated in his homeland. It stands in Paris, the gift of an American.

FREDERICK NORTH

The King's Minister

THE PRIME MINISTER OF ENGLAND, LORD FREDERICK North, sprawled on his bench in the House of Commons, gloriously asleep.

His snoring increased till it vied with the speech of George Grenville, a member of the Opposition, who was declaiming on public finance. Roused by a neighbor's elbow, North heard Grenville refer to the reign of William III.

"Zounds, sir," North protested loudly to his well-meaning neighbor. "You have awakened me a century too soon!"

Several days later a long-winded member of Parliament harangued on the utter futility of accomplishing anything while the Prime Minister slept. The pudgy North opened his eyes and retorted, "No, I was not asleep, but I wish to God I had been."

The art of catnapping as developed by North functioned

BORN: April 13, 1732, Piccadilly, England
DIED: August 5, 1792, London, England

as a Parliamentary weapon. Five days a week he lolled on the front bench in Commons, combining his snooze—feigned or genuine—with a sharp wit that punctured the Opposition time and again.

He was not an orator. His gestures were awkward, his figure flabby. His speech, which was described as "a rumbling in a mustard bowl," sounded thick, as though his tongue were too large for his mouth. His pouting lips, puffy visage, and big eyes "gave him the air of a blind trumpeter."

But the mind within the fat facade was shrewd and distinguished. A member of Parliament since the age of twenty-two, he had steadily garnered a name for himself as a master of finance and as a practiced hand in Parliamentary jockeying. George III had appointed him prime minister in January, 1770.

The King had endured a procession of middling chief advisers. His old friend "the pompous, slow, and sententious" Earl of Bute had fallen short because he lacked influence over Parliament. Next, George Grenville, a minister "great in daring and little in views," had pushed through the Stamp Act in harmony with the King's policy of chastening the colonies, but otherwise he had not proved pliant enough. Lord Rockingham followed in a brief, "lutestring ministry, fit only for summer," and then came the Duke of Grafton, whom the Opposition overwhelmed.

An outstanding Chancellor of the Exchequer for two years, North seemed the ideal prime minister. He and the King had been boyhood friends and had appeared in children's plays together at Leicester House. North's family had belonged to the peerage for nearly two centuries and had always been active in public affairs. His home life, free of scandal and filled with love of romping with his children, endeared him to the pious monarch.

Most important, North, who was not firmly committed

to any faction, could control a majority in the Commons while bending to the will of his former playmate.

During his long term in office, spanning twelve of the most important years in British history, he managed the national finances with a high degree of professionalism. In Parliament, his proper milieu, he scintillated in defense of his budget or the civil list. On familiar, domestic subjects the portly minister held his own against the Opposition's galaxy of orators headed by Chatham, Burke, and Fox.

Then the Boston Tea Party dumped pandemonium into North's lap. On behalf of the King, he asked for a sequence of acts to punish the Bostonians. These notorious bills—the Boston Port Bill, the Massachusetts Government Act, the Administration of Justice Act, the Quartering Act—passed the Parliament by virtue of North's majority sway. The patriots termed them the "Intolerable Acts" and rebelled in arms.

To nip the insurrection, England required a leader of seething, inspiring abilities. North, with one foot rooted in Parliament and the other in St. James Palace, simply could not bestride an ocean. A government supporter likened him to old dog Bosun, fat and lazy as ever. "He does very well to keep the hall and has a good tongue there, but he is not fit for the field."

Analyzing his own pugnacity, North confessed: "If a man must quarrel with me, I must quarrel with him. I will never begin, but I will never decline a quarrel."

He did not decline the quarrel begun by the rebels. More and more, though, he changed the function of his office from one of initiation to one of cooperation. With George III in the "closet," he slumped into the role of "pliant tool," accepting with curious lassitude the direction of the King's inferior mind.

North's early reputation for laziness had stemmed from his manner, not his methods. Thrown into war, he seemed suddenly bent on living up to his reputation. He dallied and delayed. Even the King grew vexed by his "love of indecision," and goaded him continually through a confidential agent in the Treasury, John Robinson.

"Mr. Robinson," wrote the King, "must today attempt his irksome part of rousing Lord North to act as he ought." The reminder was repeated over the years, varying in wording only.

"I am," admitted North, "neither soldier enough nor well enough acquainted with the country to reason upon the situation of the army." The planning of the war he defaulted to his Cabinet.

No sadder assembly of incompetents ever graced a ministry. Their phenomenal bungling sustains Horace Walpole's evaluation: "Lord Germain was of desperate ambition and character; Wedderburn, a thorough knave; Lord Sandwich, a more profligate knave; Lord Gower, a villain capable of any crime; Elliot, Jenkinson, Cornwall, mutes that would have fixed a bowstring round the throat of the constitution."

The poorly defined limits of the Cabinet would have created confusion in any prime minister without talent for coordinating national policy and the soldiers in America. North had no such talent. He frankly admitted to being unable to choose between the conflicting opinions of his ministers.

The best he ever got from a Cabinet session was a good meal. The Cabinet met once a week in the homes of the various members in rotation. After dinner the table was stripped and the business began. Along with a contented belly, North left with a pounding headache.

Although he had not wanted the war, although he pushed through Parliament measures that were not his, he managed to give the impression of the jolly fat man who never lost his temper, his capacity for sleep, or his appetite.

"Faith, my lord," he told the Duke of Newcastle, after a reversal in America. "If fretting would make me thin, I should be as sorry as your grace, but since it won't have that effect, I bear it as well as I can."

Twice he courted peace. He backed the unsuccessful mission of the Howe brothers early in the war. After Saratoga he offered "conciliatory bills" in a tardy attempt to prevent the French-American alliance. Passed despite the opposition of many of North's own followers, these bills offered to "unite the British Empire" and to exempt from taxation any colony that contributed an approved sum for internal government and the common defense.

Washington studied the proposals. He sent them to Congress with the comment that they were "meant to poison the minds of the people and detach the wavering, at least, from our cause."

For several months before Yorktown, North lived on his nerves. He received the news of Cornwallis' surrender "like a ball in the breast." He staggered back, threw out his arms wide, and groaned. "Oh, God! It's all over!"

Now he insisted on resigning, a step he had desired to take since Saratoga five years earlier. The King had always put him off: "The day of trial is not the honorable one to desert me." So North had stayed, out of loyalty and duty. There was also his "gilded chain," a matter of twenty thousand pounds by which the King had personally relieved him of his financial anxieties in 1777.

George III let him go reluctantly. "Remember, my lord," he said at parting, "it is you who desert me, not I you."

That afternoon North stood before the Commons and announced that the impending motion of "no confidence" in the ministry was unnecessary. He had a secret to disclose: the ministry had ceased to be.

The startling announcement ended proceedings far

short of the expected hour. None of the carriages of the members was in front, and the men huddled in the bitter cold and falling snow, waiting for their vehicles to fetch them.

North came out smiling. His coach stood alone. As he climbed inside, he paused and said, "I protest, gentlemen, this is the first time I have ever had any advantage from being in the secret."

The jolly fat man, who for twelve years had sometimes guided, sometimes clung to, the destiny of the British Empire, disappeared down the snow-blurred street.

Already pens were wet with his epitaph.

"The Minister Who Lost Us the War."

GEORGE WASHINGTON
The Torchbearer

NEW YORK CITY WORE A DIFFERENT LOOK. DURING MOST of the year 1783 the docks had bustled with army commissaries selling surplus firewood, wagons, cattle, and horses. Over on Queen Street, loyalist merchants had auctioned off goods they could not take northward to their new homes in Nova Scotia or the valley of the St. John's River.

On Thursday, December 4, the chance to grab a bargain was forgotten. The city teemed with excitement. General Washington walked the crooked streets.

As the clocks struck noon he made his way among the old Dutch houses and the newer ones built in the Georgian style of England. The houses stood like momentous tombstones. Buried were the bonds of politics, loyalty, and affection for the Old World. The American flag flew over Fort George.

The people hurried to line his route. Heads poked from

BORN: February 22, 1732, Westmoreland County, Va.
DIED: December 14, 1799, Mount Vernon, Va.

windows, handkerchiefs waved, and men dismounted and
pulled their horses to the side. Some in the crowds longed
to dart out and touch him, but did not dare. He was
not a figure to fondle. He tilted his powdered head and
smiled in the sober tradition of good manners by which he
lived.

Turning west on Queen Street, he gravely mounted the
curb and four steps and passed through the columned
doorway of Fraunces Tavern to bid farewell to his officers.

It was to be a moment of highest drama, even as had been
another moment at the very beginning, eight years before
in Philadelphia. Then George Washington had sat wearing
the red-and-blue uniform of his days as provincial colonel
in the war against France. The uniform silently recommended to his fellow delegates to the Continental Congress
that the time had come to fight. When John Adams had
risen to nominate a Commander in Chief, Washington,
forewarned, had not waited to hear his name. He had gone
tensely from the hall that the other delegates might vent
their opinions freely.

Afterward, he heard the details. Although unanimously
elected, he had been the compromise candidate. "I do not
think myself equal to the command," he told the Congress
in his acceptance speech. He refused to accept pay beyond
his expenses.

He spoke with Patrick Henry about his faulty qualifica-
tions. He had not actively soldiered in eighteen years. His
experience consisted of only five years of commanding small
units in wilderness fighting.

To compensate, George Washington had limitless ambition, a love of right, and since early manhood a strong
"bent to arms." He had found "something charming in the
sound" of bullets tearing the air.

"Remember, Mr. Henry," the new Commander in Chief
confided, "what I now tell you: from the day I enter upon

the command of the American armies, I date my fall, and
the ruin of my reputation."

If George Washington harbored a profound weakness,
it was this fear of public disapproval.

Walking more slowly, Washington entered the long room
of Fraunces Tavern. He moved to a refreshment table,
summoning all his stony poise to conceal surging emotions.
Awaiting his words in almost breathless silence were the
officers who commanded the troops around New York, the
last of a disappearing army.

His eyes brimmed. If he suddenly did not see the officers
clearly, a corner of his mind could not have failed to total
up those who must be absent. Gone were the almost-good-
enoughs: Ward, Schuyler, Putnam, Charles Lee, Gates,
and others who had arrived in 1775 with reputations that
dwarfed their abilities, and they had left the scene early.
Others had quit in disgust, broken by the strain of Con-
gressional slowness or by jealousies of rank. Brave ones had
died in the cause, and a few had been compelled to resign
for reasons of health.

The long room was hushed. Washington fidgeted with a
tidbit from the table. The faces watching him were a blur
. . . The exquisite boy, Lafayette, was away on a triumphal
tour of his own. Greene . . . Greene was in Newport,
straightening out his muddled personal affairs, but in war
his head had been clearest. Of the host, Greene alone with
Washington had gripped the abiding truth: the army was
the Revolution. No engagement was to be risked if defeat
meant the capture or destruction of the army. Yet in the
dark hour after White Plains, Washington had conceived
and Greene had seconded the all-out risk that dealt the
brilliant blow at Trenton.

Had Washington allowed Greene to rule him? True, the
Commander in Chief listened to the Rhode Islander's
counsel. But when the grand opportunity came at York-

town, Greene was away campaigning independently in South Carolina. Washington and Washington alone moved the army surely and rapidly to Virginia, overseeing the complexities of supply and transportation.

Other men were his superiors in intellect and military training, but none in patience, fortitude, and the willingness to learn. George Washington mastered the art of war painfully. Personal wealth and position notwithstanding, no one could lay better claim to the title of self-made man.

Now, it was time for parting. In the still room Washington abandoned the food with which he had been nervously toying. He filled his glass with wine and raised it.

His hand was unsteady, his voice faltering as he spoke. "With a heart full of love and gratitude, I now take leave of you. I most devoutly wish that your latter days be as prosperous and happy as your former ones have been glorious."

A low sound, a chorus of muffled grief, arose from the officers. They drank their wine.

"I cannot come to each of you," said Washington haltingly, "but I shall feel obliged if each of you will come and take me by the hand."

By apt chance, Henry Knox, of whom no commander could ask more in devotion and skill, stood closest. Their hands clasped. Overcome, Washington threw his arms around Knox and the two men embraced, kissed, and wept.

One by one the other officers, eyes wet and faces taut, stepped forward to receive the embrace that, having been given one, must be given all.

"The simple thought," wrote Benjamin Tallmadge, "that we were then about to part from the man who had conducted us through a long and bloody war, and under whose conduct the glory and independence of our country had been achieved, and that we should see his face no more in this world seemed to me utterly insupportable."

When the last officer had passed, Washington could bear

the sorrow no longer. He stepped to the door, lifted his arm to the group, and strode from the room.

Outside he walked through an honor guard of light infantry, down Broad Street to the slip at Whitehall. Men, women, and children thronged to the wharf to glimpse the figure rare upon the face of the earth, a man of vision who was not a visionary.

He climbed into the barge made ready to carry him on the first leg of his journey home. As it shoved off, he turned once more to the officers who had followed at a respectful distance and now stood on the wharf. Again the gesture, the arm upflung like a torchbearer, a pose wholly unintended but truly the right of the man who had kept alive the light by which others had rekindled their hope, their courage, and their patriotism.

Homeward . . . Philadelphia . . . Wilmington . . . Baltimore . . . and finally Annapolis, where Congress was sitting. Thomas Mifflin tendered a dinner. Washington came as guest of honor, though his host had been instrumental in the Conway Cabal of 1777, the shadowy plot to replace him as Commander in Chief. Washington held no resentment. Never had he permitted personal episodes to interfere with the national effort.

On December 23 he resigned his commission, "having finished the work assigned me." He had led the American army for eight stormy years, a period during which the British had changed commanders four times.

Before dawn he was in the saddle, a free citizen, relieved of his stupendous burden. Hungrily he anticipated the days ahead—days filled with picnics, clambakes, cards, billiards, fishing, duck-shooting, horse racing, riding to the hounds . . .

Even as he rode south, the trumpet of recall was rising to the lips of farseeing men. Six short years of rest and rebuilding his plantation would be his, and then, before he could rest again, the summons to eight arduous years as President. For it is a wise country, it is said, that knows its own father.

As night fell on Christmas Eve in the year 1783 George Washington cantered up the lane to Mount Vernon, bringing home to Martha and to every American the gift of liberty.

Selective Bibliography for Additional Reading

Bliven, Bruce, *Battle for Manhattan*. Henry Holt & Company, Inc., 1955, 1956. ("Minute by minute" account of a major campaign.)

Commager, Henry Steele, and Morris, Richard B., eds., *The Spirit of 'Seventy-Six*. 2 vols. The Bobbs-Merrill Company, Inc., 1958. (The Revolution as told by the participants.)

Falkner, Leonard, *Forge of Liberty*. E. P. Dutton & Company, Inc., 1959. (The story of the opening days of the Revolution dramatically re-created.)

Forbes, Esther, *Paul Revere and the World He Lived In*. Houghton Mifflin Company, 1942.

Freeman, Douglas Southall, *George Washington*. Vols. 4 and 5 of seven vols. Charles Scribner's Sons, 1951, 1952. (The Revolution from the viewpoint of the Commander in Chief.)

Guttmacher, Manfred S., *America's Last King*. Charles Scribner's Sons, 1941.

Lancaster, Bruce, and the Editors of *American Heritage*, *American Heritage Book of the Revolution*. American Heritage Publishing Co., Inc., 1958.

Montross, Lynn, *Rag, Tag and Bobtail*. Harper & Brothers, 1952.

Morison, Samuel Eliot, *John Paul Jones*. Little, Brown and Company, 1959. (The Revolution at sea through the career of the most colorful American captain.)

Pemberton, William Baring, *Lord North*. Longmans, Green & Co., Inc., 1941.

Scheer, George F., and Rankin, Hugh F., *Rebels and Redcoats*. The World Publishing Company, 1957. (Narrative account of the Revolution interwoven with letters, diaries, journals, and eyewitness reports.)

General Bibliography

Holbrook, Stewart H., *Ethan Allen*. The Macmillan Company, 1940.
————*The Narrative of Colonel Ethan Allen*. Corinth Books, 1961 (first published 1779).

AMHERST, JEFFERY
Long, J. C., *Lord Jeffery Amherst*. The Macmillan Company, 1933.

ANDRÉ, JOHN
Tillotson, Harry Stanton, *The Beloved Spy*. The Caxton Printers, Ltd., 1948. (See also under Benedict Arnold.)

ARNOLD, BENEDICT
Flexner, James Thomas, *The Traitor and the Spy*. Harcourt, Brace and World, Inc., 1953.
Wallace, Willard M., *Traitorous Hero*. Harper & Brothers, 1954.

BURGOYNE, JOHN
Hudleston, F. J., *Gentleman Johnny Burgoyne*. Garden City Publishing Co., Inc., 1927.

BUTLER, WALTER
Swiggett, Howard, *War Out of Niagara*. Columbia University Press, 1933.

CLARK, GEORGE ROGERS
Bodley, Temple, *George Rogers Clark*. Houghton Mifflin Company, 1926.

CLINTON, HENRY
————*The American Rebellion*. Ed. by William B. Willcox. Yale University Press, 1954.

CORNWALLIS, CHARLES
(Various sources.)

DE GRASSE, FRANÇOIS
Lewis, Charles Lee, *Admiral de Grasse and American Independence*. United States Naval Institute, 1945.

GAGE, THOMAS
Alden, John Richard, *General Gage in America*. Louisiana State University Press, 1948.

GERMAIN, GEORGE
Marlow, Louis (pseud. for Louis Umfreville Wilkinson), *Sackville of Drayton*. London: Home & Van Thal, Ltd., 1948.

GLOVER, JOHN
Billias, George Athan, *General John Glover and His Marblehead Marines*. Henry Holt & Co., Inc., 1960.

GREENE, NATHANAEL
Thayer, Theodore, *Nathanael Greene*. Twayne Publishers, 1960.
HANCOCK, JOHN
Allan, Herbert S., *John Hancock*. The Beechhurst Press, 1953.
HOPKINS, EZEK
Field, Edward, *Ezek Hopkins*. Providence, 1898.
HOWE, WILLIAM
Partridge, Bellamy, *Sir Billy Howe*. Longmans, Green & Co., Inc., 1932.
JONES, JOHN PAUL
Morison, Samuel Eliot, *John Paul Jones*. Little, Brown and Company, 1959.
KNOX, HENRY
Callahan, North, *Henry Knox*. Rinehart & Company, Inc., 1958.
LAFAYETTE, MARQUIS DE
Whitlock, Brand. *La Fayette*. 2 vols. D. Appleton & Company, 1929.
LEE, CHARLES
Alden, John Richard, *General Charles Lee*. Louisiana State University Press, 1951.
LEE, HENRY
Boyd, Thomas, *Lighthorse Harry Lee*. Charles Scribner's Sons, 1931.
MARION, FRANCIS
Bass, Robert Duncan, *Swamp Fox*. Henry Holt & Co., Inc., 1959.
MORGAN, DANIEL
Callahan, North, *Daniel Morgan*. Holt, Rinehart and Winston, Inc., 1961.
PITT, WILLIAM
Long, J. C., *Mr. Pitt and America's Birthright*. Frederick A. Stokes Company, 1940.
PULASKI, CASIMIR
Manning, Clarence A., *Soldier of Liberty*. Philosophical Library, Inc., 1945.
PUTNAM, ISRAEL
Tarbox, Increase N., *Israel Putnam*. Lockwood, Brooks, & Co., 1876.
REVERE, PAUL
Forbes, Esther, *Paul Revere and the World He Lived In*. Houghton Mifflin Company, 1942.
SALOMON, HAYM
Russell, Charles Edward, *Haym Salomon*. Cosmopolitan Book Corporation, 1930.
SCHUYLER, PHILIP
Tuckerman, Bayard, *Life of General Philip Schuyler*. Dodd, Mead & Company, Inc., 1905.
SEUME, JOHANN
Lowell, Edward J., *The Hessians in the Revolution*. Harper & Brothers, 1884.
STEUBEN, FREDERICK VON
Palmer, John McAuley, *General Von Steuben*. Yale University Press, 1937.

Tallmadge, Benjamin
Hall, Charles Swain, *Benjamin Tallmadge*. Columbia University Press, 1943.
Tarleton, Banastre
Bass, Robert Duncan, *The Green Dragoon*. Henry Holt & Co., Inc., 1957.
Ward, Artemas
Martyn, Charles, *Artemas Ward*. Artemas Ward, 1921.
Washington, George
Freeman, Douglas Southall, *George Washington*. Vols. 4, 5, and 6. Charles Scribner's Sons, 1951–1954.
Wayne, Anthony
Preston, John Hyde, *A Gentleman Rebel*. Farrar & Rinehart, Inc., 1930.
Wilkes, John
Postgate, R. W., *That Devil Wilkes*. The Vanguard Press, Inc., 1929.

General

Allen, Gardner W., *A Naval History of the American Revolution*. 2 vols. Russell & Russell, Inc., Publishers, 1962.
Bakeless, John, *Turncoats, Traitors and Heroes*. J. B. Lippincott Company, 1959.
Bancroft, George, *History of the American Revolution*. 3 vols. London: R. Bentley, 1852.
Becker, Carl Lotus, *The Eve of the Revolution*. Yale University Press, 1911.
Bemis, Samuel Flagg, *The Diplomacy of the American Revolution*. Indiana University Press, 1957.
Berger, Carl, *Broadsides and Bayonets*. University of Pennsylvania Press, 1961.
Bowen, Catherine Drinker, *John Adams, and the American Revolution*. Little, Brown and Company, 1950.
Bowman, Allen, *The Morale of the American Revolutionary Army*. American Council on Public Affairs, 1943.
Chidsey, Donald Barr, *July 4, 1776*. Crown Publishers, Inc., 1958.
Clark, Dora Mae, *The Rise of the British Treasury*. Yale University Press, 1960.
Dictionary of American Biography. Charles Scribner's Sons, 1928–1958.
Dictionary of National Biography. London: Oxford University Press, 1921–1938.
Donne, W. Bodham, ed., *Correspondence of George III with Lord North, 1768–83*. 2 vols. London: Murray, 1867.
Downey, Fairfax, *Sound of the Guns*. David McKay Company, Inc., 1955, 1956.
Fleming, Thomas J., *Now We Are Enemies*. St Martin's Press, Incorporated, 1960.
Force, Peter, *American Archives Series 4*. 6 vols. M. St. Clair Clarke and Peter Force, 1837–1846.

Ford, Worthington C., ed., *Journals of the Continental Congress*. 34 vols. Library of Congress.

French, Allen, *The First Year of the American Revolution*. Houghton Mifflin Company, 1934.

Fuller, John Frederick Charles, *Decisive Battles of the U.S.A.* Harper & Brothers, 1942.

Galloway, Joseph, *Letters to a Nobleman on the Conduct of the War in the Middle Colonies*. London: Wilkie, 1780.

Gibbes, R. W., *Documentary History of the American Revolution*. 2 vols. Appleton, 1855.

Guedalla, Philip, *Independence Day*. London: John Murray, Ltd., 1926.

Hamilton, Alexander, *Writings*. Ed. by John C. Hamilton. 7 vols. Joint Library Committee of Congress, 1850.

Hatch, Louis Clinton, *The Administration of the American Revolutionary Army*. Longmans, Green and Co., Inc., 1904.

Heath, William, *Memoirs of the American War*. A. Wessels Co., 1904.

Johnston, Henry P., *The Yorktown Campaign and the Surrender of Cornwallis, 1781*. Harper & Brothers, 1881.

Lossing, B. J., *Pictorial Field Book of the Revolution*. 2 vols. Harper & Brothers, 1859.

Matthews, William, and Wecter, Dixon, *Our Soldiers Speak, 1775-1918*. Little, Brown and Company, 1943.

Millis, Walter, *Arms and Men*. G. P. Putnam's Sons, 1956.

Moore, Frank, *Diary of the American Revolution*. 2 vols. Charles Scribner, 1858.

Morgan, Edmund S., *The Birth of the Republic, 1763-89*. The University of Chicago Press, 1956.

Murray, Sir James, *Letters from America, 1773-1780*. Ed. by Eric Robson. Manchester: Manchester University Press, 1951.

Peckham, Howard H., *The War for Independence*. The University of Chicago Press, 1958.

Popp, Stephan, *Journal*. Tr. by J. G. Rosengarten. 1902 (published originally in *Pennsylvania Magazine of History*, XXVI [1902], 25-41; 245-254).

Preston, John Hyde, *Revolution, 1776*. Harcourt, Brace and World, Inc., 1933.

Roberts, Kenneth, *The Battle of Cowpens*. Doubleday & Company, Inc., 1958.

Ross, Charles, ed., *Correspondence of Cornwallis*. 3 vols. London: Murray, 1859.

Schlesinger, Arthur Meier, *The Colonial Merchants and the American Revolution, 1763-1776*. Columbia University Press, 1918.

Sparks, Jared, ed., *Correspondence of the American Revolution*. 4 vols. Little, Brown and Company, 1853.

Tourtellot, Arthur Bernon, *William Diamond's Drum*. Doubleday &

Company, Inc., 1959.

Van Doren, Carl, *Secret History of the American Revolution*. The Viking Press, Inc., 1941.

Van Tyne, Claude H., *The Loyalists in the American Revolution*. The Macmillan Company, 1922.

Wade, Herbert T., and Lively, Robert A., *This Glorious Cause*. Princeton University Press, 1958.

Weelen, Jean-Edmond, *Rochambeau, Father and Son*. Tr. by Lawrence Lee. Henry Holt & Co., Inc., 1936.

Wertenbaker, Thomas Jefferson, *Father Knickerbocker Rebels*. Charles Scribner's Sons, 1948.

PERIODICALS

Edwards, William H., "Morgan and His Riflemen," *William and Mary College Historical Quarterly*, XXIII (1914), 73-106.

Gratz, Simon, "The Generals of the Continental Line in the Revolutionary War," *Pennsylvania Magazine of History*, XXVII (1903), 385-403.

Johnston, Henry P., "The Secret Service of the Revolution," *Magazine of American History*, VII (1882), 496-497.

Larrabee, Harold A., "A Near Thing at Yorktown," *American Heritage*, October, 1961, 56-73.

Plumb, J. H., "Our Last King," *American Heritage*, June, 1960, 4-22; 95-101.

Rice, John L., "The New Hampshire Grants," *Magazine of American History*, VIII (1882), 1-23.

Stevens, John A., "Benedict Arnold and His Apologist," *Magazine of American History*, IV (1880), 181-191.

Stillé, Charles J., "The Marquis de Lafayette in the American Revolution," *Pennsylvania Magazine of History*, XIX (1895), 1-21.

Stockbridge, J. C., "The Surrender of Cornwallis in England," *Magazine of American History*, VII (1881), 321-338.

Upham, George B., "Burgoyne's Great Mistake," *New England Quarterly*, III (1930), 657-680.

Willcox, William B., "The British Road to Yorktown: A Study in Divided Command," *The American Historical Review*, October 6, 1946, 1-35.

Wyatt, Frederick, and Willcox, William B., "Sir Henry Clinton: A Psychological Exploration in History," *William and Mary Historical Quarterly*, January, 1959, 3-26.

Index